# The TIMES of our LIVES

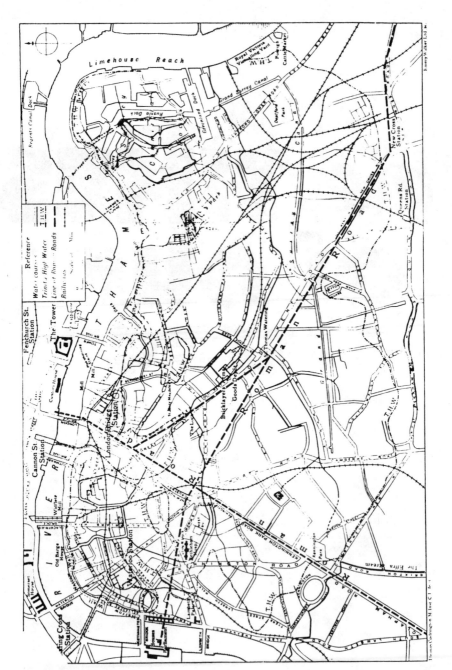

*1915 map of the approximate area covered in this book*

# Contents

Introduction                                                          *page* 4

Chapter One:
    The Environment – Sights, Sounds & Smells                          7

Chapter Two:
    The Family                                                        35

Chapter Three:
    The First World War                                               49

Chapter Four:
    Everyday Life at Home                                             57

Chapter Five:
    Outings, Treats and Holidays                                     93

Chapter Six:
    School                                                          109

Chapter Seven:
    Going to Work                                                   123

Chapter Eight:
    Monkey's Parade, Courting & Marriage                           143

Chapter Nine:
    The Second World War                                           155

# Introduction

"There's a lot of it about" – People's History, that is: not kings and queens, Gladstones and Disraelis, but history written by and for ordinary people. Since the early seventies, it has become an established part of the new literature being produced by working class writers and community publishers throughout the country, often based at community bookshops like The Bookplace.

*The Times of Our Lives* belongs to this movement. It came about like this: Peckham Publishing Project, at The Bookplace, had published several People's History books – *Looking Back*, a collection of old photos of Camberwell and Peckham, and two autobiographies by individuals – *I Was a Walworth Boy* by John Bennett and *The Ups and Downs of Florrie Roberts*. In response, many people came into The Bookplace to talk about local history. About twenty brought or sent in their own life stories. The Peckham People's History Group was formed by inviting these authors and other interested people to meet and edit another book. Southwark, our local adult education institute, helped by funding us as a fortnightly class, convened by a Bookplace worker – "convened", not "taught", because we have been teaching him.

It has taken us two years to familiarize ourselves with everyone's work and compile the extracts published here. In the first year we read each others' writing, discussed it all and agreed to divide the book into the following chapters. In the second we have decided which pieces to include from our original contributions, written new pieces to fill gaps, edited out tiresome repetitions, found the photographs and designed the book. All but three of the contributors have been able to come to meetings; the non-attenders have either been beaten by the stairs or now live too far away (e.g. Sandwich). We have kept in touch with them by correspondence.

We want to make a few points to introduce our writing. First, we would like to emphasise that this is a book of extracts, mostly from much longer pieces. The full length versions of our autobiographies are available for anyone who wants to read them. Contact us through The Bookplace.

Second, nostalgia. Nostalgia is part of the interest, for those who lived through the experiences described here. But there is more to it, as the fascinated response of young people of all cultures and backgrounds to the talks we have given in schools shows: we are talking about the identity of our area. We are not beating a drum for the "Good Old Days" – they never were good, as many of the extracts in this book illustrate. Nor do we want to encourage the exploitation of nostalgia: when a well-known TV show contacted us for anecdotes to mark the thirtieth anniversary of the last great London fog, we were unwilling. We don't have happy memories of the smog which killed thousands of Londoners over the years.

Third, politics. We have excluded direct political comments from the published writing, as we have different views and so will readers. But our meetings have often got onto the political issues raised by comparing the present with our young days. What we agree on is this: although material conditions for working class people have improved, we have no more power to control our lives. We leave you to draw your own conclusions from this and the information in the following pages.

Fourth, the historical accuracy of our memories. We decided to group the writing in chapters according to the various aspects of growing up which we had in common, instead of in chronological order. But we do not want to give the impression that the past was timeless, so we have put our years of birth beside our names so that readers can date our experiences. As for the mass of other information needed to put our memories in their proper historical context, we recommend books like "Round About a Pound a Week" (researched in South London) and the work being done by professional historians like those involved with the Ruskin History Workshop. Much research has been done and more needs doing about working class history. But these are our experiences as they were to us – People's History not only about, but, as we said at the beginning, by and for ordinary people.

# Acknowledgements

*We would like to thank the following for their help in making this book: Blackfriars Photography Project, Mary Boast, the Livesey Museum, Southwark Adult Education Institute and Southwark Local Studies Library.*

*Rye Lane at the turn of the century*

# Chapter One
# The Environment-Sights, Sounds and Smells

### Peckham
### Alice Cordelia Davis (b. 1898)

Early in the beginning of the century, some parts of Peckham were nice places to live. Peckham Road had fine houses and where the flats are built today were large well-kept houses and gardens. Towards Rye Lane the houses and shops were older but respectable and a few of the "fronts" are still the same today. I remember the Queen's Hall where now is the Ace Cinema. Next door was a large flat fronted Georgian house with a basement. This was a lodging house for men; at sixpence a night, it was called the "Woodful Chambers". From the front you could see rows of iron beds, neatly made with an enamel chamber pot on the top.

Rye Lane was, as now, a busy shopping centre; it was also known locally as "monkey's parade". The park was very popular with the young people. When I think back all those years ago, I wonder how many local people would admit to meeting their husbands or wives around the bandstand on the Rye. There were no vandals, muggers or thieving, though of course there were drunks at times. There were a lot of public houses and beer houses. Most streets had a public house at each end of the street.

Our local was called "The Alexandra"; it was large and in front it had a cellar flap where the beer barrels were rolled to the cellar below.

Next to the public house was a small carpenter's shop, where Mr Collins, the carpenter, made coffin lids, small stools and step-ladders. I remember coming home one day from school just as he came out of the Alexandra. He was a small man with a red face and bloodshot eyes. I am not certain of the correct name, but he wore a half top-hat all the time he was working. Whether it was the fresh air or the beer fumes I do not know, but he went down with a terrible crash on the cellar flap, with his half top-hat still remaining on his head. He staggered to his feet only to collapse again, his hat still firmly fixed. The noise and the sight of the man scared me and I ran home to my mother and told her that Mr Collins was dead. After I explained to her what I had seen, she said, "Oh, he is all right, God takes care of children and drunks." She was quite right, because the next day, when I passed the shop, he was busy making stools.

Next door to the public house was a jobbing builder's shop. One of the men who worked at the shop would work locally mending roofs and other odd jobs, which made him very thirsty. My mother told me his wife would not let him come into the house when he was drunk, so he would sleep in the front garden.

Most streets had their corner shop. Ours had a lovely smell. It sold paraffiin and in front of the counter were small bundles of firewood. On the counter were three large brown jars; one contained mustard pickles, one pickled onions and one mixed fruit jam. Each jar had a large wooden spoon poking out of the top; you brought your own basin and bought one or two pennyworth.

Next door was the local baker's shop where all bread was baked at the back of the shop; very nice it was too, especially the cottage loaves. With a bit of luck you might get a lovely hot roll as a make-weight. Next door to the baker's you could buy coal blocks; they cost one penny and were like black brick. I believe they were made of coal dust.

Going back to the look of Peckham, Sumner Road had a lot of very old cottages; each had a long garden that grew lots of mint, sold at a halfpenny a bunch. Hill Street also had some very nice houses. The corner still has a very old coffee shop with a dormer window. Where the Bingo is now was the Crown Theatre. It was a favourite night out, with two houses an evening; it presented mainly plays.

One sight which was very common was the pawn shops. They were almost as numerous as public houses. I remember asking my mother what the three brass balls meant. She said, "It's two to one you'll never get 'em out again." I think she was very right.

Many of the old sights and sounds have gone forever. Some are sad, some are not. I wonder how many people remember the Postman's "Rat-a-Tat"? They always knocked as the letters were put in the letter box or under the front door. The milkman too would call out "Milk Oh" as he knocked the second time with the second delivery. You took your jug to the door. The organ man too was a regular. He did not have a band organ; it was like a piano on a fixed barrow and the man turned the handle. The makers were Italian – the picture on the front was dark-haired young Italian girls. The sound was exciting. Children would follow the organ man from street to street – remember there were no cars as we know them, only carts and donkeys. They were not a great danger. At certain times of the year lavender was sold by young gypsy girls. They usually had very strong voices which carried a long way in the open street.

A most wonderful sight to see was the Fire Service turn out. The firemen wore large brass helmets, which were polished till they gleamed. The firebell was bright brass. It had a strong rope attached which the firemen pulled as the horses dashed down the road. The engine would sway from side to side. It also carried a sort of boiler which would drop ash and sparks on the road. Fires were common as there were lots of wood yards in the Old Kent Road.

I will mention one more very common sight – the funeral of a tiny baby or small child; remember families were very large. The horse-drawn cab would draw up to the house and the tiny coffin would be slipped under the driver's seat. The driver would wear a top hat with a wide black crêpe band. The followers would always cry a lot and had white handkerchiefs with a wide black band. It made me very sad, especially as I was very young when I watched these things.

## Peckham
### Leslie Piper (b. 1908)

There were some very poor parts of Peckham. Near the Alliance public house in Sumner Road many children could be seen without shoes or socks. Opposite the Alliance an Italian had an ice-cream stall in the summer and a baked chustnut stall in the winter. He also had a barber's shop nearby. Chickens used to run about the road – these, I believe, belonged to the Italian. Many of the poorer women used to wear men's caps and did their rough work in a coarse apron, made from an ordinary sack.

*"An Italian had an ice-cream stall . . ."*

I was born in a house opposite our family shop in Sumner Road, at the corner of what was then called Middle Street, but is now renamed Jowett Street. The house has gone and new buildings cover the site. Middle Street ran down to the canal, a great attraction and the source of much pleasure to us children. It abounded with tiddlers; the more scientific among us would angle for these with a worm on a bent pin and a piece of string on a stick in place of the conventional and, to us, very expensive rod and line. I'm afraid I cheated and did my fishing the easy way, with a net. We kept our catches in jam jars and were always proud if we managed to land a "redthroat"; these were considered as prize trophies, being comparatively rare.

A common sight in those days was a crowd of naked boys with their clothes under their arms being pursued by a "representative of the law". I am pleased to say that the boys usually won and disappeared into their small houses like so many rabbits into their burrows. As I look back now I don't think the police made too strenuous an effort to catch the offenders, whose only crime had been that of swimming in the canal. This was prohibited by the canal company because of the danger of accidents from drowning, but it did not stop some of the boys from diving off the bridge to retrieve coppers thrown in by onlookers.

Our branch of the canal terminated at the Canal Head, near Peckham High Street. There was a builders' merchants and a parquet flooring firm on the wharf and a waste paper contractor on the bank nearby. Many barges used the canal to bring supplies. I liked to walk along with the horse which towed them. There were a number of houses on the towpath, known as Boathouse Walk. This towpath was closed on one day each year by the Canal Company – something to do with proving ownership I think, but the residents of course were allowed to use it.

Near the canal end of Rosemary Road there was a small cluster of cottages lying back from the road, approached by a path and an iron gate. It was a very quaint and pretty place known as Castle Square, rather like Choumert Square, which still exists. There was a small forecourt to our shop; on Sunday mornings we sold pot plants, geraniums and fuchsias, mostly, from trestle tables set up there. My father had a fine T-shaped greenhouse in the garden, heated by big steam pipes. We also sold home-made ice-cream; my brother and I used to go to ice wells near the Old Kent Road to fetch a large slab of ice in a home-made cart. The shop was not a financial success, however, as, being a poor district, much of the business was on the slate and World War I brought great difficulties with getting supplies.

We moved to a private house a short distance away in Sumner Road. On some summer evenings a flock of sheep would be driven down Sumner Road, stretching right across the road; some would come in our front gate. There was usually only a child and a dog in charge of them.

Another poor part of Peckham was The Orchard – so named, it is said, because it was once a fruit-growing area, although this is hard to believe now. It was considered a rough area. It lay behind the Greyhound public house at the top of Hill Street and was inhabited mainly by costers. It was approached by Blue

*Blue Anchor Lane, Peckham*

Anchor Lane, now called Mission Place, and some of the costers used to have to lead their ponies through the house to get to the stable in the back yard.

Most of the houses in Peckham had a small garden or yard. Much activity took place there. If the yard was not suitable for gardening, many people kept chickens or rabbits; the cock crowing was a familiar sound. I kept rabbits in a shed that I had made in the garden. I kept Blue Beverans and, as a member of the local fanciers' club, exhibited animals at the local table shows.

Many people played darts and other games on Sunday mornings in their back yards. My brother and I were often in trouble through our ball going into next door's yard when we attempted to play football or cricket.

Street traders gave rise to many sights, sounds and smells which are now forgotten. The catsmeat man has disappeared owing to the shortage of horse flesh and the commercial marketing of petfood. These "Horsemeat Purveyors", as they called themselves, used to do their rounds with a pony and trolley, calling out their wares. They always had an inevitable following of feline scroungers, hoping to get the odd piece that might fall from the trolley or be thrown to them in an effort to fend them off. The cats would follow for quite long distances.

The ice man is another forgotten figure. He used to deliver large blocks of ice to butchers and fishmongers; we lads were the scroungers in this case. We would wait until the man left his van to carry a block of ice into the shop; then we would

11

*Selling salt*

raid the back of his van for any small pieces of ice lying around. There was no flavour in it of course, but I suppose it was something to suck, as we couldn't afford sweets. Most of the men employed on these deliveries were big Italians; they used to curse us – at least so it sounded to us – in their own language.

In those days, jars and bottles were not thrown away; men came round the streets collecting them. A halfpenny was the usual allowance for a clean jam jar, or a balloon or windmill for a child handing one in. One dealer I remember had a pony and trolley with a small roundabout on it propelled by hand; the children were given a ride in lieu of payment. The jam jars were used again and the bottles were sold to firms dealing in bleach and disinfectant.

The muffin and crumpet man was a regular Sunday afternoon feature of those days. He carried his wares on a tray balanced on his head and announced his presence by the ringing of a hand bell.

Late on summer evenings, as it was getting dusk, men would come round the streets with a barrow selling cheap fruit. I think they left it late so that the potential customers would be unable to see the state of their wares, which were usually beyond the point of no return. A lot of trade was done in the streets by these peddlars from their barrows. There was also the shell fish man and the one selling block salt, vinegar, hearthstone and carbolic. I don't know why these four commodities were usually sold from the same barrow, but there must have been a reason.

12

On Friday evenings in the winter we used to listen for the hot potato man calling out as he came down the road with his barrow, complete with fire, on which he baked his potatoes. Very nice they were too.

It was the days of the open fire; the firewood merchants would do their rounds, calling out "Firewood, firewood O!" Beside the chopped firewood they usually sold logs and sometimes coal blocks, these being bricks made of coal dust for keeping the fire "in", as they were slow burning. Coal could be bought at the door by the sack from the trolleyman. Most oil shops sold bags of coke, or we boys would take a home-made truck made from an old wooden box mounted on a pair of pram wheels, with two handles nailed on, to the gas works in Old Kent Road to purchase it, as I believe it was cheaper to obtain it that way.

There was no wrapped bread in my young days; we had to go to the local bakers, who baked their bread on the premises. The bread was sold by weight and each loaf was weighed before purchase. If it did not go the required two pounds, a piece of "Makeweight" would be added. Stale cakes would also be sold cheaply at most bakers and many of them made bread pudding to be sold by the piece. Bread was also delivered to families by barrow or horse van. Prices of Camberwell had many two-wheeled carts, which were a familiar sight in the district.

Milk could still be bought loose; at the dairy next door to us in Sumner Road,

*Henry Welch, a Peckham milkman*

13

there was a large bowl on the counter. Your pint or half pint was measured into your own jug. In fact, even as late as when I was at work, milk was still being delivered by two-wheeled horse carts carrying a large churn from which the milkman served his customers into their own cans. At Jordan's Dairy in Lugard Road they had their own cows until comparatively recent years. One could take one's own basin to the local butchers of an evening and purchase a hot meal of saveloys or faggots and pease pudding for a few pence, with or without gravy. Sherman's was a well-known tripe and cooked meat shop in Peckham High Street. They were noted for their home-made brawn. Most oil shops sold loose pickles and jams; you took your own container. I well remember the plum jam for its great preponderance of stones. I am certain they must have been added to increase the weight.

The main shopping centre of Peckham was Rye Lane. It has seen many changes in my time. Jones & Higgins still remains, albeit under different ownership. They used to employ two brown uniformed commissionaires to walk up and down outside. Opposite Jones and Higgins the pavement used to be built up, but this was later levelled. During a terrible national 'flu epidemic in 1918 the undertakers had difficulty in making the coffins fast enough and I remember seeing soldiers working at this job in the window of Messrs May's establishment in Rye Lane. They had presumably been released from the army to help out during the crisis.

Holdron's was another big store in Rye Lane. They used to run "clubs". My mother was a clubholder; when I started work, I had a couple of shares which kept me supplied with shirts, underclothes and other items of attire.

## Peckham Rye
### Alice Cordelia Davis (b. 1898)

Saturday in Rye Lane is a very busy shopping day and so it was at the beginning of the century. One of the main attractions was the Penny Bazaar. It was opened in 1913 at 30 Rye Lane. It was a wonderful shop, selling a large variety of useful goods. It was long, with counters each side and one at the extreme end. Many people do not realise that it was the "seedling" of "Marks and Spencer". Nothing cost more than one penny (old money).

Jones & Higgins, now the Houndsditch, was another well-known big shop, more expensive than the Penny Bazaar. Next door, on the corner of Rye Lane, was the Drovers pub. Large barrels would be put on the pavement for drinkers to sit by. Just along Peckham Road from there was a blacksmith's. I have stood very often and watched the smithy shoe horses.

At the other end of Rye Lane was the pond. The shops facing it were really very nice. It looked very much during the day like an old country village; no buses or any large vehicle would trouble the walkers.

*"Saturday night was very busy for shopping . . ." Mrs Grout's stall*

Saturday night was very busy for shopping all down Rye Lane. It was a common sight to see auction sales of meat and fish. The meat was sold off cheaply, not only the joint but a bundle of sausages and a knob of suet would be included in the deal. The banter of the butcher and crowds was comical to hear. Fish, too, was sold off – kippers, bloaters and smoked haddock, which was a favourite for Sunday breakfast. I often used to go and do the shopping for my mother, as the eldest girl in our family.

Between 7.30 and 8p.m. other important business would commence. At the pond end of Rye Lane there used to be a Chapel with a nice courtyard and a neat public house. I believe it was called the White Horse. In the forecourt of the chapel there would be held an outdoor service while outside the public house the Salvation Army would hold a very loud meeting with a very good brass band. A few yards further on a small horse and cart would draw up with a piano on the cart complete with pianist and singer who would sing and sell the latest songs. They were mostly tear-jerkers such as "Don't Go Down in the Mine Dad, Dreams Very Often Come True". I don't know why people who were so very poor loved sad songs, but they did, because the sheet music would sell very quickly. Further on another van would draw up; it was the lino man and he would sell best lino for a shilling a yard. Your fortune could be told or rather "ticked off" for one penny. These were only some of the great attractions, but my favourite was the "Foot Doctor", because I was once indirectly part of his swindle: one Saturday my friend and I helped make up the Doctor's ointment from lard and a few drops of green liquid. The "Doctor's" top hat was magic to me as I watched him make it pop-up. The lights from the oil flares and from the stalls and shops made it shine like black silk. To sell his ointment the "doctor" first had to attract his customers; he did this by using a large rattle which made a dreadful noise, so that he could be heard over the Salvation Army's outdoor meeting, the lino man and the sheet music sellers. When all was "working" full blast it was a lovely noise, but for me the best was to come.

After the Doctor had collected his audience he stood on a box which was on a barrow. He told them that, as a doctor, he had worked in North America and had cured a son of an Indian Chieftain. The Chief was so pleased that he was rewarded by being given the secret recipe for the foot ointment, from which he was made to swear never to part. He didn't: he kept it in his waistcoat pocket.

I loved to listen in the crowd. The "Doctor's" tale always had variations on the basic theme. I don't know where he came from, but as I saw him on two occasions coming from the Needful Chambers in Peckham Road, I think he must have lived there. My reward for taking part in his swindle was one raspberry cream chocolate. My mother never knew.

## Camberwell
### Lilian Blore (b. 1905)

My grandparents Lowers came to live in 1 Cheam Place, Camberwell. The landlord owned three streets of houses which met in a square – Cheam Place, Ewell Place, Caldew Street. The fourth, Sugden Street, belonged to another landlord. On one corner of Sugden Street stood a laundry where my mother worked when she was single. On the other side of Sugden Street was Miss Barker's shop and at the other end of the street was the Grand Surrey Canal. My mother said it was a small village. The village constable lived in a bungalow in Ewell Place. Every Sunday morning the men around the neighbourhood would go fishing along the canal. Before going home they would all go to the country pub, called the Boyton Arms. It stood in Boyton Row and was still there when I was born. In the hot summers the men and boys would all go swimming in the Canal. The Canal was always busy with the barges bringing the timber to the mills. It was not fenced in. The whiting barges brought up the whiting to a big yard, Jenkins'. Along the side of the whiting yard was Findlaters'. At the other

*The Grand Surrey Canal at Camberwell, St George's Church behind*

end of Albany Road was the Camberwell vestry yard. It backed on to the Addington Square Park. The vestry men took all the salvage from the houses and shops and all the salvage would be put on the barges and taken away down the canal. I can remember it being made into a coal wharf and in the World's First War I would line up for a quarter of a hundredweight of coal. That was all you were allowed to buy. In after years the yard was closed and pulled down and Addington Square Park was made bigger.

In the back streets and mews where the very poor people lived, the women always had their hair done up in curlers, with a man's cap on, an old skirt and blouse and a coarse apron, as it was called in those days. It was made from a hundredweight sack. It would be cut down and the small side cut to make one big square. Then you would cut a long piece off the side and gather it to make a band to go round the waist and put a long piece of tape each side to tie round. That was an apron. No one could afford to buy a pinafore. They had no oilcloth on their floors but would scrub the floorboards white and also the tables and chairs. They never had a lot of bedding. They nearly all had big families. They would sleep anywhere in the room where they lived. Carpets were unheard of; on the floors would be just a small rug they had given them.

My father was discharged from the Marines in the year 1900. He told us he was always glad to get home to England – there was nowhere like the sanitation and clean water to drink. My father had saved £20. No one on the ship could spend money while at sea. It paid for two gold rings – one wedding, one engagement ring – and three rooms of furniture. My mother and father were married in June 1900. They bought the sitting room sofa, a long padded seat, couch with back and raised end, one large chair for the lady and one large chair for the gentleman and four ordinary chairs all made in black material, a round table with an aspidistra plant on it, oilcloth for the floor, with a rug for in front of the fireplace, a brass fender, brass firearms, white lace curtains and a linen blind. For the bedroom there were white curtains, a bedstead and overlay, marble wash stand with jug and basin and a small table. There were no wardrobes in those days for the poor. My mother made a wardrobe out of a large cupboard in a recess in the bedroom to keep their clothes in; other than that the bedroom had oilcloth on the floor and a small rug and fender. They got a table and chairs for the kitchen and my mother bought bedding and china and wedding presents.

At the beginning of the 20th century the poor people never had no bathrooms. The gas was laid on in the streets and houses the year I was born, 1905, and a gas cooker was hired out to all the people in the house with a penny meter. It was put in the passage near the ceiling on a small platform. The penny you put in the meter would last a long time for your cooking. My mother always used her kitchen stove. The oven cooked the food lovely. She would put a kettle on the small hob and the saucepan for boiling on the big hob. The coal was only 2/- a hundredweight and there were always plenty of logs on the fire.

18

*The Baked Potato Man*

I can remember all the street cries of London. In the winter the baked potatoes man would come round the streets calling out "Large baked potatoes for a penny or halfpenny. Baked chestnuts, one penny a bag!" In the summers a man with his barrow came round. From him you could buy a large piece of salt for a penny and take a jug for one pennyworth of vinegar. Grey hearthstone or whiting was for cleaning the front steps with. There was Monkey Brand to clean the sink – a penny – and emery paper at a farthing a piece to clean the cutlery. In those days there was no stainless steel cutlery. Then there was the old lady with her basket of mint and herbs all at a penny a bunch and the fishman with all kinds of fish. He would come round the streets with his horse and cart. Around his fish was ice to keep it fresh. It was all covered with muslin. The ice cream man used to sell his cornets at a halfpenny. The gypsy had his bags of lucky heather, one penny a sprig or half a dozen pegs a penny. Once a week the barrel organ man would come to Caldew Street where he would turn a handle and the music would begin to play. The children would all dance. He would play for about 20 minutes. We never had music in our homes, so we all looked forward to the barrel organ man every Monday evening. Afterwards he would take his small bag round the street to collect some money and would leave one of the boys that lived in the street turning the handle to play the music and we would all go on dancing. The milkman would

19

come round all the streets with his small wheeled handcart with a churn of milk with measures fixed on the side. You would get a pint of milk for tuppence. The lamplighter would come round the streets to light the lamps. He would carry a long pole with a hook on the end. He would put the pole at the top of the lamp post and open the small window, lift a small lever at the side and the lamp would light. In the morning he would come and put the lights out. If anyone wanted waking early to go to work, he would tap on the upstairs window with his long pole every morning. He would get a few coppers a week for it. There were no alarm clocks then.

In Addington Square outside Cambridge House on the edge of the pavement was a long shed with a small window; inside was a stretcher with a leather belt with a hood to put up if it rained. It was used for the drunkards – they would be put on the stretcher and strapped down and taken to the police station. The police would have a key to open the shed door. My girl friends and me would come from where we used to live in Caldew Street to Addington Square. We would open the small window and look in, one after the other, fascinated, then shut the window and go home talking about it.

*The stretcher for drunks*

# Bermondsey
## Gordon Sadler (b. 1908)

I have two outstanding memories of Bermondsey. The first is the variety of smells that lingered on the air at all hours of the day or night. Foremost among these was the rich aroma which came from the biscuit factory at the end of the street. Dependent upon the wind's direction, it would ebb and flow into the nostrils, sometimes strong, sometimes faint, but always with that delicate sense of pleasure which fostered hunger in the growing child. Mingling with it, a little farther off, came another pleasant odour from a factory in Spa Road, where a well-known company produced custard powder.

Near Tower Bridge, within smelling distance of a brewery, the heavy scent of hops predominated, while from the warehouses alongside the river came the unmistakable odours of cheese, tea or coffee.

Naturally not all the smells were pleasant. A walk by the river at low tide exposed you to a stench from the grey mud, in which were embedded all the litter and oddments of wreckage left behind by the receding tide. When the wind blew off-river the atmosphere was foul.

Another noisome odour met the nostrils in Blue Anchor Lane, after passing Peak Freans'. It was the leather works and everyone made haste along the narrow pavement in search of purer air. Nearer the John Bull railway arches there was perfume in the air; a soap manufacturing company advertised its goods in a unique way – by their fragrance – and many slackened their pace as they passed in order to enjoy the unusually refreshing aroma.

Another good smell came from the tar used in the road maintenance work of those days. The roads were swept, sprinkled with hot tar and covered with tiny gravel-like stones; they were not pleasant to walk on and took some days to become embedded in the surface, but the tar remained fresh; it infused into the lungs a feeling of wholesomeness and well-being.

I believe I had an extra sensitive nose. At London Bridge I could always catch a whiff of the fruit market, which used to operate just off Borough High Street. This mingled with all the other smells of London Bridge, which in some seasons of the year were hard to define. There were hops, hay, animal foods and the rank odour of unswept streets; and interspersed with the tingling and sometimes bad commercial odours were the more cosy, intimate smells of cooking, for the whole locality abounded with tiny workmen's eating houses or cafés, where hunger could be appeased; even in the depths of war, the small coffee shops, as they were known, were rarely short of food of some kind.

A walk along Jamaica Road provided the sensitive nose with a scent-picture of this famous street. A chemist's shop – which was also a sub-post office – stood next to a pawnbroker's on a corner opposite St. James's Church; from the open doorway came the perfumed air which is always associated with scent, soap and the various compounds for preventing and healing aches and pains. Also past the

21

*Jamaica Road*

Church on the corner of St. James's Road, the open door of a public house belched forth the distasteful odour of beer and tobacco fumes. Farther along on the same side of the road, there was a corner baker's shop where baking was done on the premises and the aroma of fresh bread and cakes was a feature of that part of the road, while the window display had a mouth-watering effect on juvenile passers-by. Immediately next door was a sweet shop from which came a rich smell of chocolate; I cannot remember any time when the window was not full of loose sweets and chocolates. Without money we used to stand with our noses against the window, the sweets so near, yet so far away.

Continuing the walk, there was a large furnishing store on the corner of Keetons Road; the clean, leathery tang made a striking contrast to the other street aromas. Next, an open-fronted fish shop dominated the air; by the side of it was a greengrocer. The smells of the two shops were so unmistakable that even at night, with everywhere closed, the tradesmen's stocks would be easily discernible. Almost opposite was a florist, his small window displaying the season's blooms and his open door disclosing a perfume of arum lilies, lilies-of-the-valley and – in summer-time – the delicious scent of heliotrope.

Still farther along on the right-hand side of Jamaica Road, next to the entrance to Southwark Park, there was an old-fashioned tobacconist, who in some way was able to blend the leaf to his customers' requirements. From his door there was a fragrant aroma of Turkish and Egyptian tobaccos.

Soon after this, Jamaica Road turned sharp right into Lower Road and the borough of Deptford, but at this point nearness to the Thames once more gave a reminder of its presence.

There is one more smell I must mention. To those who lived in London during the First World War, the reek of gunfire after a night air raid was unforgettable; it polluted the atmosphere for several hours.

My second outstanding memory of Bermondsey is the variety of sounds, especially in wartime. The shrieking maroons that sent everyone scurrying for shelter and the gunfire that threatened to shatter the ear drums were part of daily life in the closing stages of the first war. Though the noise was disturbing and frightening, I am sure that most children did not realise the terrible danger to which we were all exposed. Then there were the shouts of distracted adults who, inexperienced in this new kind of warfare, were not sure what to do. These war sounds take precedence over all others and although to me there were many more "personal" sounds, nothing could obliterate them.

Other characteristic sounds came from the road-menders of the day. They used hand-tools to break the surface; a large cold chisel was hit into the ground; two men with sledge hammers took turns at banging the head of the chisel until it broke a section of the road. It was hard work; the rhythmic blows continued for long periods at a time. When the repairs had been completed, there was the sizzle of spread tar and a heavy steam roller was brought into action. In those days the steam roller was a regular part of the road-making scene and had a very special fascination for small boys. The lumbering, slow-moving vehicle would crunch back and forth over the newly-made part of the road, making a grinding, crushing noise as it travelled over the rough surface.

Living near the river it was impossible to miss the many sounds that reflected its activities. We were still in the era of the yellow fog and dark nights on the river were a hazard to those who operated barges and tugs, so that winter often brought the sound of fog-horns loudly and clearly to riverside dwellers.

There were railway arches in several streets near our home; the sound of passing trains was a familiar feature of the locality.

The L.C.C. trams were becoming a novel feature of London streets; the clanking, rumbling and hissing as they moved made the roadways appear busier than they were. The tram-driver in a hurry pounded a bell with his feet to clear other traffic from his lines. Most conductors – who evidently knew their London – called out the stopping places in a loud voice.

The single deck trams that went through the Kingsway subway were a source of great excitement to me; I remember how they whirred and whined as they ran down the slope from Southampton Row and how their little stopping stages reminded me of the Underground Railway.

But there was still a lot of horse-drawn traffic. It made a different sound to the mechanical roar of today's cars, buses and lorries. The steady clop-clop of horses' hooves on the main roads gave London an air of casualness which has long since vanished. There was less haste; the heavier horses took their time; the lighter ones trotted; and horses standing at the kerb eating from their nosebags, while the drivers were having their midday meal, were a part of the daily scene. In its way horse-drawn London was picturesque; some of the animals wore bells on their harness that jingled as they trotted; the swish of the whip – which was not often used on the horse – and the shouts of the drivers leave a mental vision of a world that has gone for ever.

*Last view of the old toll house, Dog Kennel Hill, before the trams*

## Trams
### Leslie Piper (b. 1908)

Trams first came in before the First World War, in about 1907. They became an important part of our lives and were a cheap method of travel, being operated by the London County Council. The first that I remember had wooden seats and the downstairs seats ran the length of the tram, so that you sat and faced each other. It was a great improvement when these were replaced by upholstered seats like the buses of today, except that the tram seats were reversible for when the tram did its return journey and was driven from the other end. There was no protection for the driver except for the roof; he was exposed to all the wind and rain and sometimes snow. In dense fog the trams would still keep going when everything else had stopped. It was much later when the glass fronts were added; these must have been a boon to the drivers. On a straight, quiet road the driver would stand back to dodge the rain; the tram would travel along on its own while the driver enjoyed a brief respite from the weather or struck his arms across his chest to engender a little warmth.

Trams were fitted with emergency brakes and could stop almost dead when the necessity arose. In the 1930's, during the peak hours one could travel the whole length of the route for twopence. One example of the distance one could travel was the no. 40 route from the Embankment to Abbey Wood. You could buy a shilling all-day ticket which entitled you to go anywhere, on any tram, at will; and an evening ticket was introduced by which you could travel anywhere on any tram after six p.m. for sixpence.

The tramlines were a source of danger, especially for cyclists. It took a certain amount of skill to negotiate them. Many cyclists have been killed as a result of skidding on the lines in wet weather or by narrow tyres getting wedged in them. Another danger was to horses. As a young man in 1920 I worked for my father, who was a farrier. I rode horses up Rye Lane and often the policeman on point duty had to lead my horse over the lines, as it was scared of them and would shy away, thus endangering itself and other traffic, to say nothing of me.

About that time a small solid-tyred van was introduced, known as the Trojan. These were popular, I suppose on economic grounds, but when they had to go on the tramlines in wet weather they turned sideways and often travelled quite a way before righting themselves. It must have been rather terrifying for the drivers.

The trams were usually fitted with eight wheels, but some which had to negotiate steep hills had only four, as these were better suited for hill climbing. This type, however, used to jerk and sway, so that some children would be sick. Each tram used to carry a supply of sand to be used in cases of emergency. Dog Kennel Hill at Dulwich was fitted with four sets of rails so that there were never two trams on the same track at the same time. An open topped trailer would sometimes be added to the tram on some routes; these combined vehicles were capable of carrying a large number of passengers.

When Millwall were playing at home, the trams along Old Kent Road would be mobbed by supporters who would hang all round the back of the tram and fill the footplate, wedging the conductor against the stairs. It would of course be impossible for him to collect any fares, so everyone had a free ride. A more legal concession was the workmen's fares, which were return tickets for the single fare providing they were purchased before 7.30 in the morning. In the late 1930's I travelled from Goose Green to the Embankment and back again for fourpence.

One unforgettable thing about the early morning trams was that, if you travelled on top, the air was usually thick with blue smoke, as nearly everyone indulged in either pipe or cigarette.

## Police
## Frank (b. 1900)

You had your own policeman, the same one – he never changed and you'd know where he'd be every hour of the day, which corner. We'd always call him Charlie or Harry, whatever his name *was*, that or not. The police always dealt with someone themselves. A constable never hardly arrested anyone. It wasn't heard of. If he caught you doing something, you'd both go round a back alley and he'd bring out his boxing gloves and you'd have a fight. At the end you'd shake hands and go. Mind you the copper usually won – most of 'em had hazel nuts in the gloves.

# The Street Bookie, the Look-Out and the Punters
## Harry Hawes (b.1922)

I suppose the most active occupation before the '39-'45 war and just after was that of street bookie. He and the local bobby played a very exciting game of cat and mouse in the back streets of London. There would be chases galore, ending with the bookie disappearing through a door left ajar for this purpose.

It was the job of the lookout to warn of the approach of the law. The warning, often a shrill whistle, would clear the street of bookies and punters.

The working man loved a bet, for it added excitement to an otherwise drab existence, and you would find that the local paper-shop always had a good supply of "Mid-days", newspapers which carried details of the day's racing and tips. Punters would stand on street corners, studying form, making selections and arguing over their respective choices. I recall my dad asking mum to pick out some horses, then saying they would not stand a chance, cross them out and pick his own. Needless to say mum's came home winners.

# Bugs
## Stan Hall (b.1910)

Whether we took them with us or they were already there I never found out, but I became aware of my Mother's constant battle with the bugs. Their home was the lath and plaster walls. At night they marched out in their armies to be driven back the next day to the house next door, to return the next night with reinforcements. My mother fumigated the rooms, went around the door and window frames with a mixture and stripped the beds to run a lighted candle around the spring mattress. The wooden structure was a hidey-hole for them and one could hear them popping and crackling as they were cooked by the flame of the candle.

I well remember having piano lessons on one occasion, when from under my sleeve crawled a bug. I quickly shook my wrist to rid myself of it. The rest of the lesson wasn't so much a piano lesson as a dance, as both the piano teacher and I kept moving our feet to make sure that it did not have the chance to crawl up our legs. Most people had these pests but nobody admitted to them.

# Dockland – My Playground
## Harry Hawes (b. 1922)

Our home was No. 3, Sarnells Court, Bermondsey. The entrance to the court was a small opening in the wall between Coleman's (the cooked meat shop) and the shed where Ernie the milkman washed his bottles. You went down a couple of steps and turned a corner which led to a large square with five cottages, with one outside water tap for them all. Next to the communal tap was a row of outside toilets, one for each cottage.

The court was demolished by Hitler's bombers, along with the little strangers (the bugs) who used to live with us and like the bombers came out at night.

We were lucky our house never fell down before that. It was only held up by several layers of wallpaper and a large timber prop at the front. The kitchen was very small with a copper. You lit a fire under it. Our gas cooker had a most original backplate, a large metal advert for Coleman's Mustard.

The occupants of the court were a very mixed bunch as you will see when I describe them to you.

At No. 1 lived Mrs Mead who had a local reputation as a fortune teller. No. 2 was occupied by the Manns; one of the daughters, Emmy, used to look after me. My family lived at No. 3; there were Mum, Dad (a dealporter at Surrey Docks – when he could obtain work), my young sister Ivy and myself. We also had a lodger, an old lady called Mrs Ford, who lived in the house before we moved there; she used to look after my sister and myself when Mum went out to work as a waitress at "Ye Olde Coffee Shoppe" in Parkers Row. The coffee shop was owned by Mrs Weaver, a kind lady. The Duggans lived at No. 4; their door had a glass panel which was smashed in when Mr Duggan returned home drunk – which was often. Then there were the Learys who lived at No. 5; I remember their daughter Mary had yellow fingers through working at the custard factory.

A wall separated our court from Coxon's Park in which was a vault; I was told by one of the keepers that Dr Salter, Bermondsey's first Labour MP, was buried there, but I am unable to vouch for the story.

Though I used to love going into Coxon's Park, when one particular keeper was on duty I was always chased out again. I forget what I did to offend him. I was to meet him again after the war when I called at his house for insurance premiums. He took a long look at me, shouted "Oh no!" – and slammed the door in my face (charming)!

Opposite the park entrance in Coxon's Place was a tin roofed chapel. I remember being caught smoking by a copper who gave me the choice of going to the police station or to chapel. The officer was a member of the chapel who had found a good method of getting a full congregation.

Next to the chapel was the hop warehouse; we children often watched the hop wagons loading and unloading. I can smell the hops even as I write this.

On the corner of Coxon's Place and Fair Street was Buller's, which was a sweet, tobacco and paper shop; later and until recently it was Mayne's, which before the war was run by Joe Mayne, a very nice man who showed me many kindnesses, and then by his son Wally until he sold out to the people who are in charge now.

Further down Fair Street was the local grocer's shop "Sid Jackson's"; I used to help Sid by running back and forth to the wholesalers; for that I got sixpence a week, big deal!

Next was Shephard's the greengrocer, who also sold coal and coke. I would like to tell you a story about Mr Shephard. He used to go fifty-fifty with Dad on the pools coupon. One day when Mum was in the shop Mr Shephard said to her: "Did Harry treat you out of his pools winnings?" Was she mad! It was the first she had heard about it – she never got a penny. Dad had blown the lot, £25, a fortune in those days.

Coleman's the cooked meat shop, next to the entrance to Sarnells Court, was owned by Miss Coleman and managed by Bert; he once took me swimming at Rotherhithe Baths.

The other side of the Court entrance, next to Ernie's shed, was Webb's the sweet shop, run by an elderly couple.

Further up where Fair Street joined Artillery Street was a Fish & Chip shop owned by an old lady, Miss Lewis, who kept Pekingese dogs. When the shop was closed they ran loose in the shop window – not very hygienic, but it did not seem to affect her trade.

The last shop also in Artillery Street was the draper's where if there was a farthing in the change you received a packet of pins instead (pin money.)

# A Humble Abode
## Harry Hawes (b. 1922)

How it stood up was a wonder,
that house of ours long gone,
the front shored up with timber,
the front door weather worn.

Several layers of paper,
supported walls inside;
little holes in all the doors,
where darts I threw went wide.

The fire was a kitchen range,
which mother blacked and polished;
the hearth was cleaned with whit'ning,
which the ashes soon demolished.

A piano in the corner,
on which I used to tinkle,
with knick-knacks placed along the top,
on lace which used to wrinkle.

Our wireless by the window
gave us lots of joy,
listening to the "Man in Black",
Ambrose and Harry Roy.

My bedroom was the attic,
from where I watched the train
that travelled up to London Bridge
and then come back again.

When I had the measles,
I set the bed aflame,
but Dad had some insurance,
and put in for a claim.

The bed bug was a nasty pest,
which nightly we would hunt
with candlestick and candle,
to cremate the little runt.

One night old Hitler's bombers
flew over London Town;
a bomb exploded on the house,
and knocked the bugger down.

# "Our 'Ouse"
## James Fulljames (b. 1910)

The official designation of our house was 17 Wells Place, Camberwell, S.E.5, but to me it was just "Ourouse". "Ourouse" was small. In fact, it was smaller than small. It was tiny – just two up and two down, with a little whitewashed scullery and an out-house at the back.

The frontage was only some twelve feet. There was a neat little front garden, with wooden railings and a privet hedge behind, and a small plot of grass, with a golden privet in the centre, which was always kept neatly trimmed.

There was one window up and one down. They were sash windows, each with sixteen panes of glass. Behind them were lace curtains, changed every Monday, and green venetian blinds. The downstairs curtains were looped back to display Mum's aspidistra.

A wooden gate opened on to a path of grey slate slabs, the last of which was always kept white hearth-stoned.

The front door was a cut above average, with a black knocker and letter-box, and number seventeen in shiny brass. It was grained and polished every spring. There was a fanlight above.

Inside, a short passage led to the kitchen, but a door on the left, just before you entered the kitchen, was the gateway to the Holy of Holies – the front room. Not a parlour or a sitting room. It was the front room, used only on Sundays, Christmas and special occasions like weddings and funerals. It measured some nine feet square.

The fireplace was the centrepiece. It caught the eye the moment you entered the room. It had a low open fire, a tiled hearth, a mantel shelf and a big over-mantel.

On either side of the fireplace was a recess, the lower parts of which were cupboards. The one on the left contained the gas meter, a "penny in the slot". Lighting was by two gas brackets, complete with Veritas mantles and glass shades, one on either side of the over-mantel. The cupboard had a fusty, mousey smell and in winter, when it got dark early, putting a penny in the meter used to put the fear of God into us kids. The cupboard on the right was taboo, 'cos it housed all Dad's books, which he bought down East Lane on Sunday mornings, and his collection of cylindrical phonograph records, which came from the same place.

In the centre of the room stood a circular mahogany table that tipped up if you released a little brass catch underneath. It was covered with a heavy, fringed tablecloth. On it lay a photo album and a big heavy Bible that had gilt edges and lettering. This Bible had lots of beautiful coloured plates, which we kids never tired of looking at. We were only allowed to do so as a special treat, or when they wanted to get us out of the way for half an hour. It must have been our family

31

bible, for the front pages were inscribed with names going back to the year dot. What happened to it I will never know. It just disappeared.

Three chairs with sprung leather seats stood round the table. The walls were adorned with half a dozen pictures, genuine oils, all done by Dad, who was rather good at it, and later on, two bronze plaques, "which you got for getting killed in the war".

White lace curtains hung in the window, looped back and fastened with bands of ribbon.

The walls were papered, but only the top half, the lower part being covered with match boarding, grained and polished.

A carpet was spread in front of the hearth, and another, smaller one just inside the door. And that was the "front room".

At the end of the passage was a door that opened on to a space that ran back under the stairs. We called it the "coal-hole", 'cos that's where the coalman shot his hundredweight of best kitchen nuts every Monday afternoon.

The kitchen was a trifle larger than the front room. It had a gas light fixed in the centre of the ceiling that used to shake alarmingly if you walked a bit heavy on the upstairs floor.

A large kitchen range occupied the centre of the "party" wall. It had an open fire and an oven and was religiously black-leaded once a week. The hearth was white hearth-stoned and on it stood a round three-legged coal scuttle, a poker, a shovel and a pair of fire-tongs. The fire-irons were all done with emery paper every Friday. In the winter the oven was used for cooking and a kettle stood on the hob. A long metal draught plate ran across the top of the opening to stop smoke from coming into the room; on windy days it would rattle alarmingly.

To the right of the fire-place was the dresser, with a cupboard underneath. The cupboard held some of Dad's tools and the family's shoes. The dresser above was filled with the best china, all laid out with geometrical precision, with all the cups hanging from little hooks screwed into the edges of the shelves. The top shelf was used for anything that had to be kept out of us kids' reach, such as medicines, ointments, etc. They were all pushed well to the back and you had to stand on Dad's chair to reach them.

A door led into the scullery and on the little bit of wall between the window and the door was always a coloured calendar.

Now we come to our "pièce de resistance", the table. A big square table stood in the centre of the room, covered with a heavy cloth that hung down almost to the floor. What tales that table could tell. It was used for everything – for meals, for dress-making, ironing, Dad's painting, kids' homework, model-making, card-playing . . . never was a table put to so many uses. Family, friends, relations, all, at one time or another, had sat around it to discuss their problems, their plans, their hopes. Under the overhanging cloth, its warm, dark, mystic interior made an ideal retreat for mum-nagged kids. Many an intrepid jungle explorer had

32

crouched beneath its shade, waiting with cap-loaded gun to blast the head off a fierce marauding tiger or a pouncing lion. Tiny night-gowned mums had scolded whole families of dolls beneath its solid top before being routed out by their cocoa-laden Mum and hustled off to bed. Solid, heavy, dependable. The veritable heart of "Ourouse", pulsating with family life.

In the corner by the scullery door hung a curtain, which hid from view a flight of stairs that led up to the bedrooms. A clothes rack was fastened to the wall at the foot of the stairs, on which hung the family's everyday clothes. At the top of the stairs was a small landing, with a door leading into the front room and another into the back.

The back bedroom had a ceiling that sloped down to the top of a small window. This looked out on to the back garden, the high back wall of a stables in Sedgemoor Place and a fine view of the round block of the Camberwell Infirmary. At night you could hear the horses in the stable snorting and stamping their feet.

In one corner was a cupboard that ran out over the foot of the stairs. The floor of this cupboard was some three feet off the floor and we kids called it the lobby. In it we kept all our toys and treasures and anything that had to be kept out of Dad's way. Why, I don't know, 'cos that's the first place he looked in.

Originally there was a large bed, but later on just a single one for me. A carpet lay beside the bed and underneath reposed a big enamelled "gozunder", 'cos the lavatory was at the far end of the garden and too far to go at night.

When I got too big to sleep with my sisters in the back room, I was moved into the front with Mum and Dad. I had a little bed in one corner, with a sliding curtain on an iron rail to give it some privacy.

The scullery had a sloping, red-tiled roof and a tiny window. Going downstairs through the scullery to the back, you passed in one corner a sink, a cold water tap above and a draining board that sloped up under the window and rested on the copper which was built into the other corner.

The copper was a huge affair, with a big galvanised iron bowl and a tiny fire grate under it. It was fitted with a round wooden lid, which made an ideal shield for a chivalrous knight or a blood-thirsty soldier. A little iron door was built into the wall for cleaning the flue and the whole lot was topped with a brick chimney stack and a real high chimney.

A black, iron gas stove stood in a third corner, with a narrow table between it and the copper. Over this table was a high shelf filled with pots and pans and the usual cooking utensils. Another shelf was fitted above the door from the kitchen and Dad kept some of his tools up there. A mirror hung on the wall above the sink. When we washed we used a bowl in the sink and a kettle of hot water. A coconut mat sprawled across the floor.

A door with two bolts and a lift-up catch led into the outhouse. On the back of this door was a roller towel. The outhouse had a sloping roof, half of which was plate glass. A tall wooden food safe, with a perforated zinc door, stood by the kitchen window. There was a big, heavy mangle and a galvanised iron bath with two handles hung on the wall. Another coconut mat was spread on the floor and a window box balanced precariously on the kitchen window sill.

A door led into the garden. It was a small and narrow garden running back some ten yards, with a brick path down the centre and flower beds on either side. A large wooden workshop and a lavatory sealed off the far end; both were dwarfed by the high brick wall belonging to the stables in Sedgemoor Place. A trellis screen covered with virginia creeper shielded the lavatory from view.

Other sheds came and went: one for pigeons; another as a greenhouse for Dad, adjoining the outhouse; still another as a laboratory for me, which eventually went up in smoke. But the best by far was the one we left behind when we moved in '36. It was built with a concrete floor, a large window, a skylight and a big solid work bench. It even had a lock and key – and electric light.

Well, that was "Ourouse" as I first remember it. Naturally there were changes over the years. The front room had a face lift. The old horse hair sofa was transferred to the kitchen and was used for a while as a bed for me. Its place in the front was taken over, first by a harmonium, then by a big double manual organ, complete with pumping handle, which I used to pump while brother Jack played. The ornaments on the mantel shelf vibrated; the neighbours complained; and I got tuppence for pumping. In the end it was sold to the Wesleyan Mission in Southampton Street and everyone heaved a sigh of relief.

Electric light took over from gas and the old gas stove was changed for a more modern one. The kitchen stove was replaced by a "Kitchener" and the dresser was pulled down to make way for a big moving coil speaker mounted on a huge baffle board.

Our old Edison Bell gramophone was pensioned off and a new H.M.V. gramophone with "78" records took its place.

A new scullery sink came along too, but despite all these improvements we still had to visit the Public Baths in Wells Street for our weekly tub.

# Chapter 2
# The Family

## My Grandparents
## Lilian Blore (b. 1905)

My grandmother was one of seven children. Her parents, my great-grandparents, lived in Parkstone Road, Peckham, more than 150 years ago, at the beginning of the 19th century. At that time Peckham Rye was all country and there were not many shops in Rye Lane, just some hotels. She met my grandfather Lowers at a party and started courting. After a while they got married and went to live near his parents at Nottingham Hill. They came to live at No. 1 Cheam Place, Camberwell, because her parents were very ill. My family has lived round there ever since.

My grandmother brought a son and two daughters with her to Cheam Place. She had two more daughters, including my mother, and two more sons in that house. Mothers always had their babies at home. A neighbour would always come in to help deliver the baby. It was the same in my mother's time – a Mrs Nind used to come in and help with my mother's confinements. I changed things when I had my first baby in St. Giles Hospital, although I did have my second one at home.

When my grandmother had her last child, my Aunt Maud, she was getting very bad arthritis. By the time I knew her it was so bad that three of her fingers were drawn into the palms of her hand. She never straightened them again. Both her legs got bad, as well – she could not stand.

All us grandchildren loved going to see grandmother Lowers. I always went to see her and ask how she was going on and if she wanted any errands. I always went for her errands and when I came back she always gave me a farthing for myself. You could buy a lot for a farthing then. I would go to Southampton Street, Camberwell, where the shops were. I would go to Townson's the sweet shop. Father and son made all their own sweets. There were French almond rock, pineapple stick and all different flavoured sweets. For a farthing you could get about two inches of any flavoured sweet. You would ask them not to break it up and you would keep sucking it to make it last as long as you could.

Every Monday afternoon straight from school my sister Caroline and me would go to see grandmother Lowers. All her daughters and my cousins would be there with my sister Violet – she was then a baby. They would all have tea. My Aunt Louise always brought a big seedy cake. The cake would be cut and we would all have a piece.

*Lilian (standing) with sister Caroline*                    *Grandmother Lowers*

On Saturday evenings the whole family would go. We loved the Edison Bell gramophone which my Uncle Joe bought for my grandmother so she could have a bit of music. The records were put on a cylinder and there was a small horn and a handle to wind up.

My grandfather Lowers was originally a policeman, called a Peeler after Sir Robert Peel. He was the Home Secretary who founded the police. The wages were not very much in those days in the 19th century. My grandfather was offered more money to work at Mark Brown's Wharf, by the Thames at Tower Bridge. He was a checker. He would write down all the incoming goods from the boats and then enter it all in books. He had his own office – my grandfather was very educated. He could speak many languages, including Latin, and write copper plated old English writing.

His wages when he first started work at Mark Brown's Wharf were £1.1.0. It was called a guinea in those days. He always walked to work from Camberwell to Tower Bridge. It would take him nearly an hour. He would walk home when he finished his day's work because he could not afford the fares. The houses where they lived were two rooms up and two rooms down with a back room at the back and a toilet out in the garden with a long garden. The rent was 3 shillings a week – 15p. in today's money. The neighbours grew all their own vegetables to help with their money.

At the docks they employed a few regular workers. The foreman would come to the gate and would point to so many casual workers for the day's work. They would be paid at the end of the day. The men that were not called in to work would try again. They kept coming every day, six days a week. In after years they were all made regulars and formed a union for all the workers. More work came along owing to more boats coming up the Thames and made it busier. In the winters the men were very cold. All the checkers and manual workers put on extra old coats and two pairs of socks and heavy boots.

My grandfather asked if my Uncle Jim, his eldest son, could work at Mark Brown's Wharf as well. So father and son worked together. Uncle Jim was a checker too. When my grandfather died, Mark Brown's paid all his funeral expenses and gave my grandmother a small pension until she died.

My grandfather's death closely followed by my Uncle George dying suddenly from pneumonia made my grandmother's arthritis much worse. My mother and my Aunt Maud looked after her. Her other daughters lived too far away to be much help. Aunt Maud lived upstairs in the house and used to wash her, dress her and put her in her wheelchair. This was another present from my Uncle Joe. He made it out of an armchair. He put two wheels on the back and two smaller ones on the front, a small platform at the bottom of the chair to rest her feet and a cushion for her head. He was single himself and was always very good to his mother and sister Maud and family.

My grandmother used to sit in her wheelchair in the sitting-room. She always sat by the window. That was her life for 17 years. None of her daughters could persuade her to go out. She died in 1917.

# My Grandfather
## Leslie Piper (b. 1908)

It is remarkable the years that can be spanned by family connections. My grandfather was born near Newbury in Berkshire in 1828. This was 155 years ago, in the reign of George IV, and yet I knew him quite well. He was born just 13 years after the battle of Waterloo and nine years before Victoria came to the throne. He was the son of a blacksmith and came to London as a young man. He set up in business as a farrier and smith in a forge at Canal Head in Peckham.

He was a noted character and was a great authority on the ailments of the horse; he made up his own prescriptions before the days of the veterinary surgeons. He was a friend of the great pioneer of public transport in South London, Thomas Tilling. He was for those days a well-read man and could quote from the Bible and Shakespeare. He had a large house called Vine Cottage which was in or near what was then called Commercial Road.

What is now the Peckham recreation ground belonged to my grandfather; he had 13 greenhouses on the site and grew the flowers that Queen Alexandra wore at her coronation.

I first knew him at the Canal Head, where he was still working at the age of 83.

We had an old copy of the *Daily Sketch* published in 1911 with a photo of him with his hand on the bellows handle. Unfortunately this has gone astray – but I can remember what he looked like. He had a full white beard to which he attributed his freedom from coughs as he maintained the beard was sent to protect the chest. I last knew him in Jocelyn Street where he still had a greenhouse.

His last few years were spent at Camberwell with the eldest son of his second marriage. He died there in 1918.

*Left to right: Edwin Piper (Leslie's father), George Piper (grandfather) and Uncle Harry*

*Alf Slater*                    *Alf's mother*

## My Mother
## Alf Slater (b. 1927)

She was born on the 6th June, 1884, in the reign of Victoria and Albert. Her childhood was a happy one, even though the shadow of poverty constantly hovered. There was always a deep affection when she mentioned her parents: "There was Love, a Crust of Bread and a Pair of Boots. What more could you ask?" she often said.

Her father was a milkman; she loved to relate how she and her sister used to get up at four o'clock in the morning, measure the milk into cans and help to deliver it. "We used to get ha'penny each at the end of the week for that," she said. "Still, what more could you expect, the poor old bugger was only getting ten bob (50 pence) a week to keep six of us!"

But the real prize, apparently, used to come during the deep snow laden winter. They used to deliver to a pub that opened very early in the morning. The kindly landlord would invite them in and give her father a 'Hot Toddy' and each of them a glass of hot milk and dripping toast.

These were the treasured childhood memories of a remarkable woman – my mother. I never knew my grandparents; they were long-gone before I was born. "It is a pity that you never had the chance to talk to him," she often remarked about her father. "He was a well-read man of great character and intellect." It became increasingly apparent to me in later years that this had much to do with her great capacity for patience and far-sighted reasoning.

She was married to my father on 11th December, 1905, at St. Marks in East Street; they were both twenty-one years of age. She had ten children: two were still-born; two died when very young. I was the youngest of her six surviving children – on that special pedestal reserved for the baby of the family.

My mother was of middle age when I was born. There were many large families at this time and it was quite common for women to have children well into their middle forties. This could sometimes produce some peculiar age-gaps – for instance, I had a nephew six months older than myself.

The life of women – particularly mothers – fifty years ago, was one of great personal hardship and a continual battle of day-to-day survival. To keep a family in food of the smallest minimum quantity was a daily struggle. In many families at this time, the order of food sharing was always Dad first, kids next and Mum last. And with each pregnancy and the possibility of another mouth to feed, Mum's place in the food queue lengthened.

I was born into an adult family; my two sisters were married; my eldest brother was in the army; my remaining two brothers who were still living at home were at work and contributing to the family income. I was therefore comparatively shielded from the many privations and hardships that my brothers and sisters had endured. When – as my mother often said – she had one in her arms and five others clinging to her skirt, the only thing they had to eat was "Air Pie" and a few "Skimps". This was an old saying which meant nothing to eat.

My love and admiration for my mother were always something special. I realised from a very early age that she was in constant pain; her right leg was badly ulcerated. No one in the family was ever allowed to see her dress that leg – it was always done in private. But however hard she tried, the intense pain she was suffering was always evident. In those days of "Do-It-Yourself" medical treatment, it was simply a matter of, as she so often said, "A case of grin and bear it".

The births of babies were all carried out at home; it was almost unknown for a woman to have a baby in hospital. There was always a "Mrs So-and-So" in every street who would act as the unpaid midwife and dash round at any hour of the day or night to assist in a birth. Clean linen, hot water and a kind-hearted neighbour, these were the only ingredients that women had to cope with their many pregnancies . . . The death rate among new-born babies at the time was appalling.

My father died when I was about seven years of age; my few memories of him during those last years of his life are good ones. I was the only child in the house and fairly reasonably spoilt. When I was being particularly awkward, he would raise his hand and stop and walk away. My mother told me in later years that he would say, "I would like to but I can't forget". This was a reference to the fact of how he had thrashed my brother just a week or so before he died from diphtheria. However my mother felt the loss of that child, her great gift of compassion would emerge in defence of my father: "I'm sure he didn't know how ill he was". I never knew this brother; his loss explains the age-gap between myself and the rest of the family. "That helped to change him for when you came along", she said. Then she would laugh and add, "And of course, your brothers were getting older and learning to throw righthanders as good as him." I knew exactly what she meant about the "Righthanders"! My brothers and sisters had often related to me the many stories of the hard and brutal life my father had made them all endure when they were children. The many beatings that he inflicted on my mother as she attempted to protect them from his drunken rages had given them a feeling of revulsion and an undisguised hate. He was – and is even now – always referred to by the cold detached title of "The Old Man".

My mother's courage was always obvious to me from a very early age. I never ever needed to be reminded of this by my brothers and sisters; it was something you were born to recognise. But as the years progressed, it was her humour, her compassion and above all, her wisdom which came out as well. These special qualities were constantly in use as, virtually single-handed and almost totally house-bound, she guided me with patience and understanding through the difficult period from boy to teens and subsequently to the stage when she would so often say: "Keep your heel and toe firmly on the ground and never let your mother say she bred a jibber".

Many of these very fine qualities she possessed were evident whenever she related some of the episodes from her earlier life to me in later years. It was to her everlasting credit that the thing she hated most was always used as an excuse and never the reason.

"It was the drink, yer know", she always started like that. "He wasn't too bad when he was on the straight; he used to stop in for a week sometimes. He still had a drink though, cos I had to make a rota for the other kids and one of them had to stay in every night to run back and forth to the 'Sultan' with the jug. Then he would just sit there and F . . . and Blind . . . mostly at me. Yeh, it was a lot more peaceful when he was on the straight."

She would even extract some humour out of this, as her small, finely etched face suddenly broke into a smile and whe would add: "Still, that's better than feeling like one of Jack Dempsey's punch bags".

Shortly after my father died, we moved from Sultan Street to Sears Street. This was a considerable up-turn in our environmental surroundings. We moved across Camberwell Road, but it was as if we had crossed an environmental frontier – "Ain't it a change not seeing any cod's heads or dead cats in the road", said my mother.

One of my brothers borrowed a coal lorry to move us. "We're moving in style this time", she said. "The last time we moved your father was in the army. He went on the 'Trot', so they stopped my money. We owed so much rent that we had to get a pram and do a 'Moonlight' one night round to 'Buff Place' ".

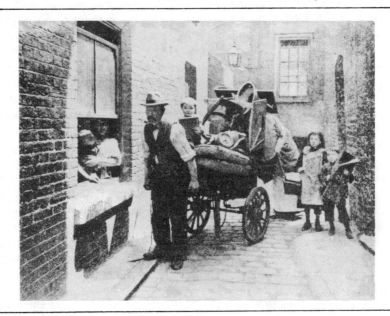

*"Doing a moonlight . . ."*

*Sultan Street, Camberwell – Backs of houses*

Although my mother was a widow, she was not entitled to any pension. My father was a "Totter" – as a self-employed rag and bone man he had never bothered to buy any insurance stamps. She would have been almost destitute; the only other means of financial assistance available was that obnoxious means–testing charity called the Board of Guardians. But at this particular time the need for the cap-in-hand treatment wasn't necessary. My two brothers were still at home and contributing; it may not have been a large amount, but having spent most of her life scrimping and scraping, she was a financial wizard with the smallest amount of money.

Her leg was steadily getting worse; she was having to use "Old Gus" more and more. "Old Gus" was the name she had given to the crutch that she had to use – there was always the joke and the humour. The windows became a very important part of her life; the kitchen overlooked the garden and the front room overlooked the street. Through the many months and years of painful confinement to the house, those two windows became my mother's view of the world outside.

My brothers eventually married and moved from the house, I was now alone at home with my mother. The subsequent lack of income necessitated an appeal to the Board of Guardians' for assistance. The weekly visit by the man from the Guardians with his charitable pittance, quizzing eyes and prying information was a further test of my mother's character.

With just the two of us, it was considered that the half-house we had in Sears Street was too large. We moved to a small compact flat in Evelina Mansions. The war had just been declared and then the Blitz started; the horror of the bombing and the interminable hours spent in the shelter were endured by my mother with the same brand of courage and inspiring confidence that was hers alone. "We seem to be like the Drury Lane lady, always in trouble," she would say.

The war ended and within a few years a whole new concept of advantages were available to her: an independant financial dignity and medical treatment for her leg. But at seventy years of age it had come too late: the leg had to be amputated. She accepted this with the same quiet courage; it was just another obstacle in the path to the future.

She recovered and learned to walk again with a false leg.

For the next five years she enjoyed an independence and a personal freedom that had seemed unobtainable . . . but alas, all too late.

At seventy-eight she died in East Dulwich Hospital.

So ended the life of a wonderful and remarkable woman . . . my mother.

# Dad
## James Fulljames (b. 1910)

Dad, christened Henry George, was always called Harry. He was around five feet nine, slim, wirey, with grey hair and moustache. Of neat appearance, even in working clothes, always with collar and tie, and his boots were polished to perfection. I know, 'cos I had to clean them every night, thoroughly – for which I got tuppence a week.

He suffered from arthritis in his hands and one knee, which Mum said was the Lord punishing him for his cursing and swearing and for going down East Lane on Sunday mornings when he should have been at the Mission.

He smoked a pipe, stuffed with Skipper tobacco, which used to stink so much that he was obliged to do his smoking at the back door. I can see him now. In those days we seemed to get more summer storms and he revelled in a good storm. There he would stand, leaning against the back door, puffing away at his pipe, with the rain pelting down, with thunder and great flashes of lightning, calling on the good Lord to "Send it down David", which used to worry Mum no end, in case the Lord took umbrage and had him struck by lightning.

He was a painter and decorator by trade, doing most of his work in the West End. Our own house was done from top to bottom every spring and the little skill I possess is entirely due to his instruction. The passage, front room and kitchen were match-boarded half way up and every spring they were rubbed down, stained, grained and polished. A craftsman. They don't make 'em like that any more.

He did lots of painting in his spare time, both in water colour and in oils; some of his work must still be knocking around in the family.

He played the mandolin, a popular instrument in those days, but his arthritis made it difficult to finger and he changed over to the banjo. He taught both brother Jack and I to play and when we three got going Troise and his Mandoliers had nothing on us. The girls too would join in with paper and comb, with the tin whistle, or with the "submarine" – a wierd contraption shaped like one, with a little disk of tissue paper that produced a buzzing sound when you blew through it.

At one time he played the dulcimer and he could coax a fair old tune from a one-string fiddle which he made from a big cigar box. Even the bow was hand-made by him.

He was a great one for "putting the curse" on people. During the Great War, food was rationed and the Ministry of Food was run by a bloke called the Food Controller. Well, he must have done something to upset Dad, 'cos he promptly put the "Curse of the nine black cats" on him; and Dad's reputation as a putter on of curses went up by leaps and bounds, 'cos the poor chap very obligingly died two weeks later.

He reckoned that he could swear in sixteen different languages and, judging by some of his horrible utterances, he probably could.

He could not be termed a religious man, but he did go to the Mission on Sunday evenings to keep Mum company. Not that it did him much good. He would return home and plant himself in his armchair, with his arthritic leg stretched stiffly out in front of him; we kids would go barging around, knock into his outstretched leg and bring down on our heads all the curses and swear words imaginable.

He was also a great one for taking oaths. He must have moved house several times before settling down at "ourouse", for he took a solemn oath and swore by all his gods that the next move he made would be "feet first through the bloody front door". He was subsequently proved right, for he died of pernicious anaemia in the old Camberwell Infirmary and was brought home to await burial in the Camberwell New Cemetery at Honor Oak.

He was strict with us kids at meal times; woe betide anyone who started to natter whilst eating. He would give the culprit one of his "perishing looks" and they would be struck dumb. Another thing was Grace. At dinner, when we all sat down together, no one ate until Grace had been said. Nothing elaborate. Just a simple "For what we are about to receive may we be truly thankful". No mention of God or the Lord, so who we had to be thankful to was a matter of individual choice. Grace was only for dinner, never for any other meal.

Well, that was our Dad. Our "Farver". I can see a lot of him both in me and in mine and have no doubt that more will be manifest as time goes by.

# We Were Seven
## Jim Allen (b. 1915)
## *and* Knights of Old (a poem)

The year 1930, the house small: two up, two down, with an outside toilet in a small back yard. The call of nature at night was answered by the use of a chamber pot underneath the bed. No privacy, no solitude where one could be alone and think – and dream. I would at times climb on to the roof and lie on my belly to escape the claustrophobia that engulfed me. I needed room, space for physical and mental expression. There were six brothers, three older, three younger. I was in the middle, a buffer.

I was fifteen and had been left school a year. We slept in the one bed, three up, three down. The eldest was like a father figure and a kind of discipline was instilled automatically. Those older than you knew more, those younger relied on you – I was in the middle. My father slept in a small bed in the corner; ours was a bigger bed by the window. My mother and sister Ethel slept in the next room.

Having no bathroom and no privacy is bad enough for a young lad: for a girl who was the only female apart from mum it must have been hell, as there were times every month when privacy was required – she had none.

Ethel was the eldest of the family and worked in the kitchen basement of a coffee bar in Fleet Street. She would often walk to work and back, because, although fares were cheap, she just did not have enough money to take a tram. After a time she changed her job for one that paid a little more. From this meagre sum she managed to pay a deposit on a piano and found the five shillings a week hire purchase.

It was a Barnes piano and cost the enormous amount of £50. It was kept locked in the front room – the parlour – which was a space reserved for visitors or a funeral parlour when someone like my Grandad died. I would sometimes creep into this room, open up the piano and touch the notes with one finger. No one in the family could play, but at times Ethel's friend would entertain us with a rendering of "Fire", to the amazement of us all. From my one finger exercise I managed to progress and now today I bore people to death with my attempts at numbers like "Makita", "Tondelayo", "Ramona" and "Girl of my Dreams". I've earned a few pints from this as it is nice when I stop. Ethel is responsible.

One of my brothers, John, was not a strong lad in the physical sense, but he had moral fibre. Although not as fit as others he did manage to join the Territorials along with George, the oldest brother. Their drill hall was in Abbey Street near Dockhead and they were both in the boxing team. George, now disabled, was at that time considered to be quite useful with his fists. At that time John, like Ethel, worked in the kitchen of a restaurant and that meant he was rather late coming home – not the best of jobs for a lad of his nature. It was on one of his late nights that he was chosen to box at the drill-hall. It was an eliminating contest, which meant that he had to fight three bouts and win each fight to qualify. He'd worked late, almost run all the way to the hall and could easily have been excused without loss of face. To his credit he fought and won two of the fights; but the third was too much for him and he lost. What a heart-breaking moment for a youngster! But he took it with a smile, as he so often did.

Once, in later years, when I visited him in hospital, he said, "Jim, you looked a picture walking down the ward – a real picture". I had just returned from a holiday in Wales and wore light casual clothes; I had caught the sun and must have looked good. John was dying. When he did go, I wore those same clothes at the funeral.

Bill, younger than John but older than me, was a scalliwag. He would, if he could, get out of all the household chores and pass them on to me. I was younger, you see. Being younger, I thought that he was always right and would obey without question for a time. There was one occasion when he woke me very late at night. It was dark, cold and still. The rest of the family were fast asleep. Downstairs in the larder was a blue paper bag, the type that grocers used to fill up with sugar and sometimes prunes. We often took a couple of these to eat now and then. On this night Bill woke me and in a soft voice said, "You awake? Shhh, don't speak. Just listen to me". I listened. There was a sense of urgency in his tone.

"What is it?" I whispered back.

"Shhh! Now listen: you're lighter on your feet ain't you; you are more quiet." I nodded. "Right then, get out and slowly creep downstairs and you know the cupboard? On the middle shelf by the bread bin – you'll see some prunes in a blue bag. Now keep nice and quiet – you can do it. I want you to open the bag and get a couple and bring 'em back to me; you can do that, can't you?"

"Yes, Bill."

"Take one for yourself" – and he gave me a pat of encouragement.

"Cor, thanks!" I said and like a fool I crept downstairs in the cold darkness to do as he'd instructed me, feeling proud to know that I'd been entrusted with such a dangerous mission and being grateful for the one prune that I could pinch for myself as a reward! He was a rascal, but I managed to catch up with him in time – that is another story.

Space prevents me from telling all I would like to tell about my sister and my brothers. Sufficient it is to say that I owe a lot to them – whatever I am. Apart from John, they are still around: George, a bachelor, the eldest, with pacifist views and a strong desire to change society; Bill, Bob, Len, Stan, myself and of course Ethel (keep the best till the last) are all married, all grandparents. All were involved in World War II: we are fully paid up members of society. Believe me if you will when I tell you that my brothers are gentlemen, and my sister – a gem. I am privileged to have been one of the family – I wouldn't change my name for a million pounds. We are still seven.

Postscript – Saturday, December 11th, 1982: I have just received the sad news that Bill has passed away – last night. No more will he play his little tricks on me, but if the one of his many escapades which I have mentioned in my tale has brought a smile to the face of the reader, then he hasn't lived in vain. I would dearly love to be able to creep downstairs tonight to pinch a couple of prunes for him – and take one for myself. Thanks, Bill.

# Knights of Old

They were six in a bed
Three up, three down.
"Goodnights"had been said
And quiet was the town.
Near each little face
There were two little feet,
Secure in their place
Until body heat

Caused the small one to turn
The big one to itch
As the temperature rose
To fever pitch.

Those in the middle
Had no respite:
It was shove, push and fiddle
For most of the night.

Those next to the wall
Had to fight to get free,
To get past the rest
When they wanted to wee.

The ones on the outside
Would start to complain
When those close to the wall
Had to crawl back again.

There was moans and groans
And cries of "Oh no!"
Then twelve little ears
Heard a voice from below,
    "Get to sleep!!"

*Six little heads*
*Settled down in the gloom*
*Three up, three down,*
*And quiet was the room*
    *'Til the bugs came out.*

# ChapterThree
# The First World War

## We Just Did Not Understand
## Gordon Sadler (b.1908)

The experiences of the children of World War I were vastly different from the children who lived through World War II. In the First War, although the bloodshed and the dangers were very real for the adult population, children lived in their own homes, went to school and carried on much the same as children in any preceding generation.

There was of course no radio or television to pinpoint the horrors of those years and few boys and girls were interested in reading the newspapers. The war was remote; we only thought about it when someone we knew came to school wearing a black armband – a father or a brother had been killed. There was a war going on in France; we heard our elders talking about "The Front", but it meant little to us as we scrapped, romped and kicked our paper balls about the playground. It was a natural thing to us when young male teachers disappeared and were never seen again; all we knew was that they had been "called up" – we never quite knew what that meant.

We sometimes wondered why food was not so plentiful; but we were used to making do with what we could get. For example, unheard of today as suitable for human consumption, but much sought after in the 1914 War, was a cod's head, which Mother brought home at rare intervals. It was a grotesque-looking object and the flesh was insipid and full of small bones, but it was a change; we dipped our bread in the liquid and enjoyed the new flavour.

Like most children, I was fond of sweet things and when jam was not available, Mother sometimes produced a tin of condensed milk, which she spread on slices of bread and which we eagerly consumed. Sometimes the little corner shop would have jam – of a kind – and it was usually dispensed in small quantities; if a customer took her own container she could buy a pennyworth or even two-pennyworth of this war-time jam. I remember it was quite late in the war when some real jam came into the shop; it was tinned quince from South Africa and had a most wonderul flavour. I have never to this day tasted any jam quite so delicious. We never gave a thought to the fact that much of our food came from overseas and that thousands of men were working on the sea to make sure that it reached us.

I remember seeing wounded soldiers in blue uniforms, but it did not strike me in any way unusual; it was a familiar sight. In my mind there had always been men in blue uniforms – I was too young to have known anything else.

The women in black we sometimes saw screaming in the streets were to us figures of fun. How were we to know the great tragedy that had come into their lives, the death of a husband or of a dear relative, "killed in action". Generally, children were not unhappy in those grim and bloodthirsty years. We just did not understand.

## Zeppelins and Haddock's Ears
### Dick Piper (b. 1908)

I was almost six years old when the 1914 war broke out. The days that followed seem at this late stage to be composed of school and food shortages and the nights of fear during the air raids.

At the outbreak of war we had a small sweet and tobacconist's shop in Sumner Road, Peckham, and here it was that I experienced my first air raids. I would crouch in the recess by the side of the fireplace in the kitchen and remain as quiet as a mouse until the all clear. One bad time was when an aerial torpedo seemed to pass overhead with a terrible rattling noise. It dropped in Albany Road near the Old Kent Road and did a lot of damage, causing many deaths.

The air raids were announced by police riding round on bicycles with placards on their chests, blowing whistles and shouting out "Take cover". Later we had the maroons. The Zeppelins were the first raiders. I saw one come down in flames. It was brought down at Potters Bar. Men would climb the lamp posts and smash the gas lights, although generally the blackout was not so strictly enforced as in the Second World War.

Meat, I believe, was rationed except that if you had the money, a bit extra could always be found. I used to have to queue for potatoes and a pail of coal, sometimes without success, as often the supply was exhausted before my turn came.

We sometimes obtained what we called "haddock's ears" from the local smoke hole (fish shop) and a piece of hard cheese from the provision merchant to augment our meagre food supply.

Our ink at school was made up as required by mixing a powder with water; it was more like mud than ink.

German tradesmen, many of whom must have been here for years, were badly treated and I remember a German baker near us in Rosemary Road having a brick thrown through his window.

Apart from the shortages, the air raids and the occasional wounded soldier in his blue hospital clothes, the war was very remote to us children; or, perhaps because we were young, we didn't understand the terrible tragedy that was being enacted as the adults did.

# Losing a Brother
## Stan Hall (b. 1910)

It was after the summer school break when I was transferred to the "Big Boys"; I wasn't so much transferred as thrown in. It was also the year that saw the death of my brother. I joined the ever-increasing numbers who had lost fathers, brothers, uncles and cousins.

The air-raids made people take cover under the stairs; unfortunately we were unable to do this as under our stairs was the coal, which although cheap, was wanted for the war effort and was precious. We joined forces with a friendly family opposite our home. There were a few bombs dropped; being the first raids ever to be experienced by ordinary people, they were very frightening; the mother of the family displayed great fear by rushing about and screaming. My mother, made of sterner stuff, did not like to see her family upset by such women and found another shelter – in the cellar of the Albany public house on the corner of Cunard Street in Albany Road. Here, although many people were congregated, the licensing laws were relaxed and people became braver by keeping their "spirits" up.

One night during our visit to the cellar, the Germans launched from a Zeppelin an extra large bomb; some even called it an aerial torpedo. It landed on a block of flats on the corner of Calmington Road in Albany Road, some 200-300 yards along from us. The noise was terrific for those times and pieces of debris from the explosion landed with force on the cellar flap of our shelter. That experience caused my mother to change shelter again, to the mineral water factory of Rawlingson's, which backed on to the Surrey Canal near our house. As their output had been cut because of the war, the stocks held in the cellars were very small, their daily produce moving on the same day as it was produced. There were some 200 people who used this shelter; if a bomb had ever dropped on that place many lives would have been lost.

It was in this year that the dreaded telegram came to say my brother was in a hospital in Berkshire. Not knowing what had happened to him, my parents went as quickly as they could. Had he lost an arm? A leg? His sight? He had in fact contracted "Trench Fever" so badly that he was paralysed. He spent some weeks in hospital, but did not recover and died. He was just 18 years old. He was buried in our local cemetery in a communal grave for service-men, those that had been lucky enough to return, but not survive. On the morning of the funeral a gun carriage and six soldiers arrived and his coffin, which had been delivered to the house, was placed on the gun carriage. A Union Jack was draped over it and with us in horse-drawn carriages (cars were not in use yet for funerals), we set off for the cemetery. There, after the lowering of the coffin, shots were fired across the grave. I believe the government supplied all this pomp to try to convince people that their sons and husbands etc. all had this type of burial, when in fact bodies were blown to bits and many covered by the explosion still alive. One of the worst jobs in those days was the poor messenger boys'. They had to deliver the fatal telegrams, as indeed happened in the Second War: at the mere presence of a messenger boy in your street many hearts stood still.

My brother had joined the army because he thought each family should make a contribution – and better him than his father. As he was a surgical instrument worker, the army put him into the Army Medical Corps. The friend with whom he had joined – they had hoped to stay together – was put into an infantry regiment. I missed my brother very much. My mother, of course, not only suffered the loss of her elder son, but also missed the large contribution he had been making to the household.

The war years meant hours of queuing for the small amounts of food that were available. Mothers even queued outside a shop on a rumour that there might be a delivery of something; it mattered not what it was, anything was acceptable. It was some years after the war before this state altered. Men came back to no jobs, some having been "gassed", others without a limb and those that were blind would not be engaged; there were few jobs and plenty of reasonably fit men.

## Spit and Scratch, but never War
## Alice Cordelia Davis (b. 1898)

The saddest thing I can recall was when the 1914 War was declared. Nearly all the young men went. They were the brothers of my school friends, all with whom I had played Snakes and Ladders and Ludo on their kitchen table, before their mothers and fathers came home from work. We used to play by candlelight and when the candle was burnt down to the candle grease we had to watch it burn. We never seemed to get burnt – my mother used to say, "God takes care of children". These fair boys all joined the army to "Save England" and nearly all were killed; some, too, were sailors. In one family there were four brothers and all were drowned.

When you think of these horrors, anything is better than declaring war. Spit and scratch by all means, but never war. The Camberwell Gun Brigade was so very sad. I watched them march off to war. So few came back. All were good brave young men, but I doubt if they knew what it was all about.

*Southampton Street (now Way)*

## Shrapnel and Clinkers
## James Fulljames (b. 1908)

If an air raid looked like being a bad one, my family would drag me along by the scruff of the neck to take shelter in the deep cellars under the Bun House in Peckham Road. Quite a few of the locals went there. Others, particularly the old 'uns, preferred to take their chance under the kitchen table, with a mattress on top as an added precaution.

The day following the raid, all us kids would be out in the street digging up shrapnel from the tarry block road. Bits of iron, old nuts and bolts, nails, it was all shrapnel to us, to be treasured and gloated over or exchanged for fag cards at a later date.

I remember Armistice night – the dancing in the streets and the big bonfire they lit, which was so fierce it damaged the road; the next day a horse and cart came along and the road collapsed, leaving a huge hole. I can also remember a Zeppelin being brought down in flames and everyone out in the street cheering like mad.

During the war, Samuel Jones, in Southampton Street, changed over to making munitions, or some other war work. Whatever it was resulted in great heaps of clinkers outside the boiler house. On dark evenings we kids would load our pockets with clinkers and engage in pitched battle with kids from a neighbouring street; many a kid went tearing home with a nasty bump on his head or a cut face, hollering blue murder.

# Air Raids, War Widows and the Bastille
## Lil Blore (b. 1905)

The World's First War started in 1914. I was 9 years old. My father was made a Special Constable for the firm of Epps Ltd. and other employees were made constables. They had to report in turn to do duty and watch the firm that no damage was done when the air raids were on. My mother was left with three children when my father was on duty at work. My mother was expecting her fourth baby. My sister Alice was born in 1915 in the same bedroom as my sister Violet and I were born. The war was getting very bad by then. A bomb fell in Albany Road, October 1914, killing 10 people. The plaque is still on the wall of a house there, as a memorial for the dead. The first sailor to be killed in the war was Mr Fox who lived next door to where we lived in Caldew Street. His ship was called HMS *Amphion*. It was mined. Mrs Fox was left with two children. There were no air raid shelters in the First War. We had maroons to warn us that the air raid had started. If it was night time my mother would take us to the Boyton Arms public house. All the neighbours would come too and go down the cellar. When the raids were over the maroons would sound the "All Clear". The Boy Scouts would come round the streets on their bicycles with "All Clear" on the front of their bicycles. We went to the public house because it was a much stronger building than our house. It stood in New Church Road, Camberwell.

My Uncle Joe went into the army. He had to sell his business. He had no one to mind it. My Aunt Maud was left a war widow. Her husband, my Uncle Charley, was one of the first to be killed. She was left with four children. She lived with my grandmother. My Uncle Joe, her brother, was very good to her, as she looked after my grandmother. My Aunt Maud was given a war pension and Uncle Joe paid her so much a week and clothed her children. But when he went into the army he was given a shilling a day, seven shillings a week. He would send home five shillings to my grandmother. They had to live on his five shillings and Grandmother's pension that she got from Mark Brown's and Aunt Maud's war pension. Six people to live on that money (approximately 13/6d)!

In the war years and before the First War, widows wore "weeds" with a large black hat. It was made of tulle and would cover the face. The black clothes would be down to the ankles. The widowers wore a black arm band round one arm for a year and a black tie.

The Rev. Percy Herbert was always the first to offer his condolences to the widows or fathers and mothers who had lost someone in the war or anybody who had lost someone in an air raid. He was liked by everyone. He was vicar in 1916 and years after became Bishop of Norwich. All the vicars and reverends have all worked hard for the people in Camberwell Parish.

When the war was over in 1918 it was very depressing times. There was no work for all the men who came out of the forces. My Uncle Joe was very lucky. My

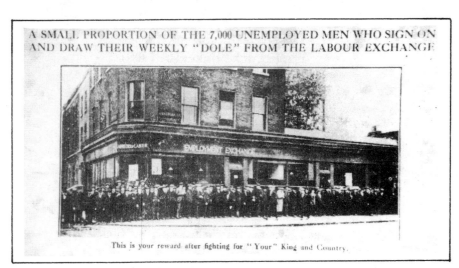

A SMALL PROPORTION OF THE 7,000 UNEMPLOYED MEN WHO SIGN ON AND DRAW THEIR WEEKLY "DOLE" FROM THE LABOUR EXCHANGE

This is your reward after fighting for "Your" King and Country.

*Pre-election newspaper advertisement, 1924 (?)*

Uncle Jim, his brother, asked Mark Brown's Wharf (later Hayes' Wharf) for a job and he started as a checker. A lot of people went into the workhouse from 1918 to 1930 – they could pay no rent; they had no money. Some of the husbands went and broke up stones at the end of each day. They were given so much money for their families. The Gordon Road workhouse was nicknamed "The Bastille".

*"The Bastille" – Gordon Road Workhouse*

# God Send You Back to Me
## Trixie Packe Baker (b. 1909)

When the war started in 1914, one didn't know what to expect in the way of air raids, yet needed to be prepared in some way. So Father put pails of water beside the fireplaces.

Men went through the streets, blowing whistles of warning and calling out "Take cover!" Then, it seemed to Trixie, all the neighbours in her block of flats came pouring into the front room, where the faint hearts knew her mother had a small bottle of brandy hanging on the bed post for emergencies. They would all chat or moan until they heard the whistles blow again and the men calling "All clear!" Then they would slowly make their way home again. Trixie's two brothers were in the army and she would sit up in bed, singing "God Send You Back to Me", which was the popular song of that time.

The aeroplanes could be heard droning overhead. One bomb was dropped on a small baker's shop in Walworth Road, the next turning to Deacon Street near the Elephant and Castle. A lot of damage was done on a Saturday morning elsewhere.

When Armistice Day arrived, 11 November 1918, the chief thing Trixie remembered was the party a woman gave in the block for a lot of soldiers and her husband coming home unexpectedly. A fight followed amid screams and the sound of furniture being broken.

# Chapter Four
# Everyday Life at Home

## Being the Eldest Daughter
### Alice Cordelia Davis (b. 1898)

This was life for me in London at the turn of the century. I was the eldest child in a family of nine. I remember so many of the details because my mother looked to me for help. This state of affairs was almost the same in each house; there was nearly always a "big sister" whom the younger children looked up to. Our large family was normal for our time, but sometimes out of seven or eight children in a family, two or three would die of "fever", so my mother said.

As the years went by, my sisters and brothers arrived; usually I woke one morning to find we had a new sister or brother. My youngest brother was born when I was twelve years old. I remember his birth so well. In those days, nearly all were born at home. No doctor, but a "monthly nurse" was booked. She was called "monthly", but her job was to look after my mother and the baby for ten days. I remember our lady; she was always very busy. She was very clean looking; she wore a white apron with a bib. The part I remember most was each evening she would sit by my mother's bed with a jug of porter, which was a type of black beer. She would chat to my mother and enjoy her drink, which left a dark brown rim around her mouth like a moustache. I do not know how much she was paid for looking after my mother, but I do remember seeing a few golden sovereigns in the bottom of my mother's chest of drawers.

My brothers and sisters loved each new baby. My mother was not a big woman, but she always had lovely babies. Years after, when I was grown up, she told me that she had looked forward to the ten days' rest. Toys and dolls were very rare to us girls, but I do believe in the "law of compensation", because we always had a live doll to love, fuss and feed. When I think back to my childhood, today's unisex fashions are not very new because little boys wore petticoats and wore their hair long until they were about three years old. Little Lord Fauntleroy tunics with lace collars were very popular, also sailor suits.

My mother used to do all the washing herself. We had a "copper" which was in the small scullery. At times it smoked; so to overcome this, my mother would send out for a halfpenny worth of gunpowder. She would put it in a roll of paper and push it up the front of the fire. We all rushed out to the front of the house to wait for the bang. Of course it duly came, followed by a blue flame. It cleared the chimney, but how it did not bring it down I do not know.

My mother did her best on a very small amount of housekeeping. She used to make a good dinner for us when we came in from school. There were always plenty of good vegetables and sometimes she would make a large raisin pudding. In those days, suet did not come out of a packet and a large lump went into puddings. Her meat puddings were out of this world. She did not believe in gravy, salt, colouring or anything artificial.

When we returned home from school, we used to go straight to the dresser, which was in the kitchen. Placed in a row, there would be pieces of carrot, turnip or apple, and, very rarely, a boiled sweet. We all had very good teeth.

My mother did not believe in fancy soap. I used to get a bar of Sunlight soap; it was two large bricks of soap joined in the middle. When twisted it would break into two. All washing was done with it, including us children. Our hair was washed with it and we all had wonderful heads of hair and good skins. The only member of the family that was not washed with Sunlight soap was the new baby. My mother would put a handful of oatmeal in its bath water.

My mother was our doctor. If our bowels were out of order, liquorice powder was prescribed; it had a most revolting taste. A spoonful was mixed in water, when it would turn a nasty greeny-grey colour. A box of this powder would cost one penny. Pills were sold in little round boxes with a red rim, but my mother did not believe in these. For pimples she prescribed brimstone and treacle, which was mixed in a jam jar. The black treacle was nice, but the sulphur was a bit gritty, though tasteless. The pimples could not stand it. For sore throats, a piece of flannel was put around our necks and we were made to gargle with salt water. For chesty colds it was Russian tallow. A large piece of brown paper was well smeared with the tallow. It resembled creamy-yellow candlegrease. This paper was put across our chest and back and tied on with a warm scarf; we were then put to bed with a cup of warm milk. For a cough, mother prescribed glycerine, paragoric and syrup of squills: this was mixed in a medicine bottle at a cost of five (old) pence. For a feverish cold a dose of quinine was recommended. This was taken in water: it would turn the water milky white and was dreadfully bitter. All these things seemed to work.

My father was a man of his time. He would buy a large sheet of leather and mend all our boots. I would watch him put "brads" (small nails) in his mouth as he held the hammer in his hand. My father's pleasures were very few. He was a retort repairer at Greenwich. I do not know exactly what he earned. I do know it must have been very hard work. It used to burn his hands; I've seen his lovely strong hands scarred through burns. The skin on the palms was tough as burnt leather. The words "unsociable hours" and money for "dirty work" had not been invented. I doubt if his wages were more than £3 a week, but I never heard him complain. He used his bike to go to work. His hours were long and included Saturday morning too.

How did our parents manage to clothe such a large family? It certainly was at times a big problem – and our large family was just the average type of London working family.

Boots were the biggest worry. My father would take us to a boot maker's and the workman would measure our feet. We would go the next week to collect them. The price was 4/11d a pair and they were leather; plastic had not been invented. We had a neighbour who had a larger family than ours; two lots of twins added to her troubles. What she used to do was declare war on the landlord and refuse to pay the rent. With the money she would buy childrens' boots and pay back one shilling a week on her current rent. She was the loser in the long run, as her landlord was the same as ours and he owned about six houses. He had a "rich" sister who passed on to my mother her child's outgrown clothing and toys, story books (Grimms, Hans Anderson – lovely books) and games. I never met this "rich" girl; I asked my mother about her. My mother said "She is Genteel but one of "Pharaoh's lean kind". It was my mother's genteel way of saying the girl was thin. Of course this only happened now and again. My mother paid one shilling a week into a clothing club. It did help; we always seemed to look nice and tidy. The genteel girl was no good to me as I was not genteel – the opposite really; but I loved the story books and games.

In those days you had dresses made by a local dressmaker; she would charge about 1/9d or 2/6d to make a dress. You supplied the material, which would cost about 8¾d a yard. I learned at a very early age to make do and mend. I could make a simple dress, also underwear. I shall be laughed at about the underclothes. I could make a nice pair of shrimp-coloured flannelette drawers with embroidered lace at the knees. Oh yes! But it was the fashion and even then we all liked to be in the fashion; we were quite happy.

In my young days most working men expected to provide for their families. Mothers could not go to work because most were having their children. Many people were worse off than my family. I have seen children going to school in the winter, barefooted, with very poor clothing and very thin; and I have seen where they have been ill-treated. All shops would sell canes for beating children; they were like a very thin walking stick. They were cruelly spiteful. I have seen arms and legs with criss-cross weals and I have seen children faint in the classroom. Of course I did not understand what I saw. There was fever and all sorts of illnesses: ring worm, skin diseases . . . Most were caused by malnutrition. I have seen drunken men fight other men – and women too. A child looks at these things as a spectacle.

Beggars, cripples and blind men were very common. Although my mother did not have anything to spare, she always seemed to find something for the "poor devil". Sometimes it was two slices of bread and dripping for a beggar at the door; the cripple or blind man would get a few coppers as well. My mother used to say, "I don't like my withers wrung". Exactly what "withers" are, I don't know, but I think it must have been the kindness that was wrapped up inside the bread and dripping, or the few coppers.

People had very little help from the State in those days. There was only private charity. In Peckham we had (I think it still exists) a large house which was called The Settlement. This house was paid for and run by our local church; they did a wonderful amount of good work for the homeless. A lot of poor old ladies lived in little back rooms with a small Beatrice stove for heating and cooking, with a halfpenny candle for lighting. The good ladies from the Settlement used to visit the old and sick and bring them warm petticoats and flannel drawers to keep them warm. One of these good women was called Sister Mabel, who not only cared for her fellow beings but also cared deeply for animals. I can see Sister Mabel as I write; she was a tubby little lady who wore a nursing sister's uniform, a black straw bonnet with streamers and a wide silver belt. She was always accompanied by her little tubby dog.

The Settlement was a God's Blessing to all kinds of people. For example, when a confinement was expected, a bag of bedclothes would be lent to the expectant mother, or soup would be sent to the new mother. Many a great kindness was done for the "girl in trouble". It was a very common thing to hear that May so-and-so or Jane so-and-so was "in trouble". When the gossip, oohs and ahhs had finally stopped and what my mother called "the poor little blood" finally arrived, things got back to normal. The little one would be absorbed into the poor girl's family as one of the natural brood – and do you know it was always a most beautiful child. My mother used to say, "A love-child is always beautiful" and "God always sends them food and love". Think that one out and see how right she was.

These times were very sad and horrible, not "good old days", although the state of affairs was not general. As I have said, you found a great many homes were like mine. I always think there is a reason for everything; and one thing I insist on is that people were not dirty or shiftless. Remember bathrooms were rare in small houses and bedding was very poor. Straw was used to fill mattresses. It all caused vermin; overcrowding too – I have seen families who lived in one room.

Men did get drunk. I do not excuse this, but they came home after a very hard day's work; a baby would be screaming in a pram in the kitchen; the men would go out as soon as they could, to get drunk. This is a very depressing story, but it is all true. My "withers" feel deeply wrung. Most of these things I hope have gone for ever.

My family not having a lot of money, we always had a lodger. This helped with the rent of twelve shillings a week. I mention this because it was the first time I had heard a gramophone. The recordings were on cylinders and he would play the same tune over and over again. I remember the tune well; it was called, "When the Fields are White with Daisies"; this was preceded by a nasal voice saying "This is an Edison Bell Record." It sometimes used to run down with a deep moan, then come up slowly, then gallop.

We always had a parlour, which was my mother's pride and joy. It was the custom in those times, when anyone died, to lay them in the parlour so as the neighbours could come in and see the body. The door was kept shut, as no children were allowed in. When Bill, the lodger, died, he was laid in the parlour. I was always a very forward child, so during the week he laid there I was determined to see for myself. When all was quiet, I crept down to see – and I did. The lid was just open past his neck. He looked asleep, but so white and so clean. He had a curl on his forehead which I had never seen when he was living. After my inspection I went back to sleep. I did not feel any fear.

As I got older I was sent out to the local park with a large pram, a baby at each end and some others toddling beside. On my way to the park, Mrs Smart or Mrs Hill would ask if Willy or Little May could come, so in the end a small cavalcade would go to the sandpit. One day, after a morning out, we returned home to discover one had been left behind. It was my sister Grace. I returned to find her playing quite happily with other little ones.

*"In the end a small cavalcade would go to the sandpit . . ."*

*"I was not a goody goody child . . ."*

I did my duties as the eldest daughter, but I was not a goody goody child. I knew a large grocers who sold 3lb jars of jam, costing 11d (old pence). The big attraction to me was on return of the empty jam jar you got a penny; well a penny was untold wealth to me. One skill I had was I could make a good fishing net. We lived very close to the canal, so, with my brothers, something had to be done. In our front garden we had two rather sad-looking plane trees. If you carefully selected a branch, pulled all the leaves off, found three hair pins, two large strong ones and a portion of net curtain – with care and luck, some strong button thread and a jam jar (the neck of the jar would need a strong piece of string) all would be ready for the "fishing", which was also a gamble as a large notice on a board said "No Fishing Allowed". The bank on the opposite side was a standing place for a wood yard – what a grand thrill the local boys had pushing wood into the water. The old chap who was in charge could not manage to care for about five barges (all drawn down the path by a very large horse); so of course the swimmers would make straight for the barges and push the planks of wood off. The wood was like skirting board planks.

Here is a story about the canal. I came home from school one day and my mother was in tears. I said, "What's the matter?" She said, "Henry William has been missing for two hours". I said, "Oh, he is all right, he is playing with his friends". She said, "No, I'm sure he is drowned". Well, I knew, as young as he was, he was all right. He could swim as well as the others, also run (which was a great asset) as fast. My mother said in her tears, "Will you find him?" My first call was at the canal. The only corpse was a swollen dead black cat and a few planks, so as I stood looking and wondering what to do, I thought of the police station, which was close by. Where I stood was at the Peckham end of the canal, and I was about four minutes from Peckham Police Station. When I arrived at the station (I believe the building is almost the same today), I went up the front steps into the office. I suppose you would call it the shock of my life to see a policeman sitting at a large desk without his helmet – to add to my surprise he was bald on top. When I recovered from my surprise he asked me kindly what I wanted. While I was asking if he had a "lost boy", my brother, I glanced round and there in front of me was Henry William, sitting on a backless form with a cup of lemonade, two biscuits, three boiled sweets and a bar of chocolate. Well, I was so surprised, but my brother knew what I knew. He had large innocent blue eyes, a mop of what my mother called flaxen hair and a dirty face (which helped him) – so after I had told the policeman my brother's name and address (the rogue knew as well as I did!) and we were well away from the police station, I did my bit of judging. I said to him, "You know what will happen if you do this again?" He said, "No." I said, "They will send you to prison" (I wonder what a 4½-year-old convict would look like). He was cured – I helped him eat the chocolate. His had a piece of string stuck to it, but mine was all right. We both went home and ate our dinner.

Have you ever been told not to do something? Usually it is for your own good, especially if you are a child. But why does that order or request make you want to do that forbidden thing more than ever?

My mother told me never to go into a public house or go into a pawnshop. A youngish person would not know the meaning of a pawnshop. I will try to explain what a pawnshop was like. Poor people, and some not so poor, would use these shops to borrow money. I have seen customers lined up waiting for the shop to open. I think most would know each other well and really enjoyed the gossip with each other as they waited. The parcel each one carried was usually a very tight little bundle secured with a pawnshop pin which was very long and straight (about an inch and a half). I carefully watched this from the grocer's shop when I shopped for my mother. The pawnshop itself was a corner shop. I examined the shop when the door was opened. It was not a large shop, but the counter had three small partitions, why I do not know, as I am sure each one knew what was in the other's bundle. In the corner behind the counter was a chute and as the man examined the contents he would write out a strong little brown ticket, put one half on the bundle, give the customer the other and then throw the bundle into the chute. When it was filled, he pulled a rope and up would go the bundles. The usual term for this was "going up the spout".

As I stood watching, the bundles arrived on the floor above, which was filled with racks. A young man stacked them neatly in the racks. So now you can understand why the tight bundles and strong pins.

The other part of this shop had a large notice which said, "Unredeemed Pledges For Sale." There was a motley collection of clothes and small ornaments, also fire irons and flat irons.

The public house at the corner of our road was also forbidden to me. Sad to say I longed to go in it; this is how I managed. In my very young days, public houses sold vinegar in large barrels. No child under fourteen years was allowed in. However, as soon as I was fourteen, I made for the public house to buy some vinegar.

A child hears all sorts of things and mostly believes all they hear. To my childish mind I had heard public houses called Gin Palaces; to me this was connected with kings and princes. Remember, the one I was thinking of was called the "Alexandra" and she was a queen.

About my vinegar visit, I excitedly went in the "Jug and Bottle Department". The first thing I discovered was the doors did not have handles; you pushed with your shoulder. The door itself was two doors and to come out you pushed the

About my vinegar visit, I excitedly went in the "Jug and Bottle Department". The first thing I discovered was the doors did not have handles; you pushed with your shoulder. The door itself was two doors and to come out you pushed the doors open each way. Either way would push you in or out.

My next inspection was a large room with saw-dust on the floor and four revolting small pots on the floor in front of the counter. These were called spitoons.

In the passageway were long mirrors with large coloured printing saying "Jamaica Rum", "Indian Pale Ale", "Irish Whiskey" and "Oporto Wines". I cannot say I was impressed one way or another – in fact a bit disappointed. The only fairy tale bit was the huge gas lamp outside which was very ornate, lit by gas.

As I went home with my vinegar the air was much sweeter than the "gin palace".

When I first started work, as a child of fourteen, I was a bad influence on my sister. With my tips from work I would buy a large box of face powder at sixpence and a small box of rouge. Sometimes on a Saturday evening my mother and father would go for a walk and I would be left in charge. With the help of a small mirror in the kitchen, we had such fun with that make-up. However, we did not have any eye make-up so we decided to make some for ourselves. Here is the recipe. First you must spit into the palm of your hand, burn two or three matches and then crumble the ash into the spit. Do you know, it was very successful. Mind you, we did look a bit as though we had been out in a fog.

The biggest sin I committed was to buy a packet of five cigarettes, I believe they cost twopence. It was a green packet and the name of them was Wills. Sometimes we would buy a ha'porth of sherbet powder which made two cups of wonderful fizzy drink. We loved it when it tickled the back of your nose. To us this really was the wild life.

Another "crime" I committed was in my reading matter. I had been told at school never to read trash; well, sad to say, the first time I had a spare penny I bought a yellow backed novelette. I was so disappointed; although it was a love story, I thought it so silly. One part said "He crushed her to his manly chest, breathing deeply". I thought it sounded as though he was "chesty".

But now that I am talking about work and love stories, I am beginning to leave my childhood life at home behind . . .

# Baths – "Out"
## Stan Hall (b. 1910)

We had Baths in Wells Way, quite close to our home. For 3d. you were supplied with a small square of soap and what appeared to be a length of corrugated paper (they said it was a towel). You paid your money and received your ticket at a small pay box, Men's one side and Ladies' the other; in fact the man and woman issuing the tickets sat side by side but peered through different service holes. I always wanted, as a cheeky young lad, to go to the Ladies' window, just to cause a diversion.

Inside you handed your ticket to a man in overalls, who appeared out of the steam. You were in a large space with cubicles of black stone, open-topped. They seemed to be made of black marble. The attendant would lead you to one of them. Inside was a large bath of the same colour as the cubicle. On the floor was a wooden linked mat. The attendant would use a key to turn on a tap outside and a flow of water would enter the bath.

The attendant knew the correct amount of hot and cold water that would supply the measure required. You of course were not the only person receiving his attention; shouts could be heard for "A drop more hot for No. 6" or "More cold in No. 13" etc., as well as the curses should cold be turned on where hot was wanted. What with the yelling of the inmates for their water and their curses, plus the heat and steam of the place, a bath was anything but relaxing. Under the Baths was the wash-house, where mothers could bring their weekly wash; for 1d. or 2d. they had use of a sink and the supply of hot water, also a wringer to remove most of the water before taking it back home to dry. To do the washing in this place you had to be prepared to stand in a couple of inches of water, because a collection of mums would be at work and water would be splashed everywhere.

# Baths – "In"
## Lilian Blore (b.1905)

My mother and father and us four daughters went out to the baths in hot weather, but in the winter we never went. We didn't want to catch cold coming out into the streets after having a hot bath, so we bathed at home. Having no bathroom, we would lock the scullery door, put a large saucepan of water on, heat the water and put it in a galvanised tin bath. Then we would put the saucepan back on the fire with water for the next person.

Every Friday night when we came in from school we girls had our baths in front of the fire. Our hair was washed, thoroughly combed and plaited up for the whole of Saturday, to be undone on Sunday. My eldest sister had the first bath, then me. Afterwards we always had a dose of liquorice powder.


# Chores
## Leslie Piper (b. 1908)

Of course we had our chores to do. Some of mine included turning the handle of the mangle on washing days, cleaning the knives with a saucer of wet brick dust and a cork and the eternal errands: a pennyworth of potherbs for the stew, a half mile walk for a bottle of loose Parazone for washdays, a similar distance to pay Dad's slate club at a pub in Hill Street and fetch back an ounce of St. Julian tobacco were some of my regular shopping orders.

When we could, we took our hoops with us on errands. Hoops would be virtually impossible to use today because of the road traffic, but in those days most of us possessed one. The girls' hoops were mostly wood and were propelled by hitting with a stick, while the boys' ones were usually of iron and controlled with a hook known as a skimmer. I had a fine hoop and a strong skimmer, my father being "in the trade". I was quite expert with these. I could run in among the people on the pavement without touching anyone and stop immediately, no matter how fast I was travelling. My father was a farrier and blacksmith and repaired many a broken hoop for the boys by fire welding them. I think he charged twopence for this.

Our copper in the wash house sometimes required blowing out. I loved this job, as when we had a good fire going, my mother would wrap some gunpowder in brown paper, open the fire door, then hold it firmly with a broom. There would be a big bang, which I loved to hear; this apparently effected the necessary clearance.

# Sundays
## James Fulljames (b. 1908)

Sunday was different. Best clothes, Sunday School, high dinner and tea – and no playing in the streets.

If you went regularly to Sunday School you got your name down for the annual outing to Ashtead Woods and you built up quite a collection of little coloured texts which said, "Blessed are the meek", "Jesus loves me", or "God is love", which you could swap with other kids like you swap fag cards.

We went to the Wesleyan Methodist Mission in Southampton Street. There were three services on Sunday: morning, afternoon and evening. We kids went to the afternoon service. There was a Bible class too, during the week, and a Band of Hope, but we liked the Bible class best, 'cos they showed lovely coloured slides on a big magic lantern.

The head of the Mission was a Mr Mitchell, who seemed old to us kids. He had a sweet factory in Parkhouse Street and one of his special lines was Mother Mitchell's Cough Drops. They were a well known local product, on sale in most sweet shops. He had a son called Wesley, who played the Mission organ, and Mum didn't like him much 'cos he was always skylarking around with the older girls and making faces at them in the organ mirror. Also he drank a lot and had a boozer's nose, with lots of little red lines on it. Or so Mum said.

The Sunday School superintendant was a Mr Mallet, a suitable name, for he was a cabinet maker and a good one too. He lived with a genteel old couple named Thurgood. Mrs Thurgood, a dear old lady who always wore a black bonnet, was my Sunday School teacher; she often, after school, took home a couple of us boys to tea. I liked going there 'cos they had lots of books on shelves and after tea I used to look at them. Now and again they'd let me borrow one to take home.

There was another lady teacher named Miss Savage. She worked at Jones and Higgins; I thought she was a smasher and could never understand why she married Mr Mallet, 'cos he was much older than her. Dad said it was Mallet's beard that tickled her fancy, 'cos he had a pointed grey beard and looked a bit like a picture of Jesus Christ.

Harvest Festival was the time we kids enjoyed. The whole of the Mission platform would be loaded up with great heaps of vegetables, fruit and big golden loaves. All these good things were eventually auctioned off and the money given to the poor.

Dad reckoned it would be better to give them the goods instead of money, 'cos half the buggers spent the money on booze.

We always had a Christmas Tea, with a magic lantern show afterwards. There was never any shortage of washers-up after these teas, 'cos all the cakes and fruit left on the dishes were given to the washer-uppers to be taken home as perks.

Every year they held Revival Meetings and people like Gypsy Smith used to preach; lots of poor souls used to kneel at the penitant form, confess their sins and be "converted" in front of all the people. Some of the audience used to get real worked up and jumped to their feet with cries of "Hallelujah" and "Praise the Lord!" Mum was always trying to get Dad to kneel down, but he got out of it by saying that "If he knelt down with his gammy leg he'd have to stay there till bloody Doomsday".

On Sunday evenings, when Mum and Dad were at the Mission, we kids, that is Ivy, Emm, and I, used to sit around the kitchen table and amuse ourselves in various ways. Painting, raffia or making up models of farm-yards and cottages from sheets of coloured cut-outs that we bought from Smith's paper shop in Wells Crescent. They were only tuppence a sheet and were good value.

We were not always so well behaved. Sister Emm was fond of a smoke; as cigarettes were out of the question, we did the next best thing and rolled up dried tea leaves in bit of tissue paper and smoked that. The stink was something awful and it's a wonder we survived.

On one occasion, instigated by me, we decided to be "Kentucky Minstrels". We tied a piece of cloth on a stick, and poked it up the chimney to get some soot. We dressed ourselves up in some old coloured curtains and bits of cloth and blacked our faces with the soot. We looked real good, especially sister Emm, who had nice white teeth, 'cos she cleaned them regularly with soot mixed up with salt. We performed. We sang and we danced and must have lost count of the time, 'cos right in the middle of "Swanee River", in walks Mum and Dad. On their own, it wouldn't have been too bad, but they'd brought back with them a couple of old people from the Mission for a snack and a little chat. Well, they were livid, that is Mum and Dad were, but the old couple seemed to think it funny and could barely keep a straight face. Ivy and Emm got a real ticking off over it, but I got off scot free, 'cos I was the youngest and had obviously been led astray.

# Sunday School
## Joan Leamy (b. 1913)

Memories of Sunday School during my childhood are centred on the school run by the Church of God at Clayton Hall, a big two-storeyed building in Peckham High Street on the site now occupied by the Odeon Cinema, almost opposite The Bookplace, near the bottom of Rye Lane.

Crowds of children from the neighbourhood of Sumner Road and the streets around gathered on Sunday afternoons, the younger ones in the big hall upstairs and the bigger ones in classes downstairs. My grandfather, Mr W. T Champion, was the first superintendent I can remember, followed later by my father Mr

Albert Leamy and then a gentleman called Mr Silver. Each of these was helped by teams of teachers, about ten at any time, and they all faithfully taught us the Bible stories, helping us to understand God's love for each of us, shown by sending his son to die for us. I should think that every boy and girl learned that text which has been called "The Gospel in a Nutshell" – St. John, chapter 3 verse 16: "For God so loved the world that He gave his only begotten son that whosoever believeth in Him should not perish but have everlasting life".

Sometimes the teachers would give us "Object Lessons" (using what would now be called "Visual Aids"). Either they would bring along an "object" to remind us of a Bible text or they would ask us children to produce something for them to talk about. For example, we could take five small stones to remind us of what David picked up out of the brook and how he chose one and put it in his sling when he killed the giant Goliath. These lessons could produce some laughter as for instance when a child brought along a sausage to illustrate the text "Behold, I show you a mystery!"

An extension of the work of the Sunday School was the "Thursday class" when the children gathered in the evening for similar teaching but in a more informal atmosphere. More of the "visual aid" methods were used here and it was quite a thrill when we had a "Magic Lantern" show. Books such as *Pilgrim's Progress*, *Christie's Old Organ*, *Jessica's First Prayer* etc., were illustrated in this way. Sometimes the apparatus would not work, causing much amusement, but that still happens today with the more sophisticated film-shows.

Some children remained in the school from a very early age, five years or younger, until well into their teens. Others unfortunately thought they were too old when they reached thirteen or fourteen. When one little girl was asked why her big brother had stopped attending, she said "'E can't come to Sunday School! 'E smokes, wears rubber 'eels and 'e's got a girl!"

# Sundays
## Alice Cordelia Davis (b. 1898)

Our Sundays were very nice. My father always had his breakfast in bed and read the newspaper. After breakfast all of us children (except the last baby) would be prepared for Sunday School: us girls with a nice hair ribbon and hat and the boys with nicely parted hair. The most important thing was our boots had to be well cleaned and shiny. As each of us were ready we went up to my father for his inspection. He always examined our boots first. His greatest words of praise to each of us were, "You look a real toff". My mother always said, "What did Dad say?" Off we would go for the eleven o'clock service. We were mostly fair haired and blue eyed and must have been a pleasing sight to our parents.

As we came home and opened the front door for our Sunday dinner, we were greeted by the lovely smell of a freshly cooked caraway seed cake. This cake would be placed in the centre of our Sunday tea table. Sometimes we would have some watercress and in the winter time there might be a head of celery. Our food was plain but very wholesome.

My religion was well grounded – I tried all the Sunday Schools. I went once to a Catholic Sunday School; I had heard there were confessional boxes, where I thought I would be able to wash my slate clean of all my sins. Unfortunately I was unable to understand some of the ritual so I returned to my old Sunday School, the Chapel in Rye Lane.

The Chapel was very full on Sunday night; it was warm and cosy and I enjoyed the singing of the wonderful choir. In those days the chapel had side light fittings in small clusters. I am sorry to say my mind and eyes would wander around the congregation. There were round pink bald heads and each face had a long white beard, mostly nearly to the waist. Many would be asleep. Suddenly they would wake with a start and shout, "Hallelujah", or "Praise the Lord!" which would set them coughing. I watched a kindly sides-man bring around a small tray of pear drops to pass to the sufferers. I tried a small cough, but I was not offered a pear drop.


# Sundays
## Harry Hawes (b. 1922)

A typical Sunday at 3, Sarnell's Court, Fair Street, Bermondsey in the thirties would start with Dad sitting up in bed playing "O Sole Mio" on the mouth organ, for when Dad was awake nobody slept.

During breakfast a poorly dressed man regularly came to the Court singing for money. Sometimes a timid knock at the door revealed a person collecting money for a relation's funeral, so the poor soul could avoid the stigma of being buried by the Parish.

Just before twelve o'clock Dad would be off to the pub, rolling back after closing time.

After dinner Mum and Dad would go to bed and I would go to Sunday School at the Union Congregational Church behind Tower Bridge Police Station. The Sunday School was run by Sister Lottie who split on me for spending the collection money on ice-cream.

Tea would be celery and winkles, which we had every Sunday and what a din the family made eating it! I never liked anaemic rhubarb, so I listened to the music they made while I did my winklepicking. I enjoyed eating the little fellas but hated getting them out of the shells and taking their hats off.

Sunday tea over, Dad would be off to the pub again and sometimes Mum would go with him, which stopped me going out to play; I had to look after my young sister, Ivy.

# Children's Games 1900-45
## Compiled by Betty Colman, Alice Cordelia Davis, Harry Hawes, Stan Hall, Alf Slater and Winnie Slater

You will not see kids today playing football with a bundle of rags tied with string, bowling a hoop along the street or enjoying themselves with a whip and top. Our scooters were pieces of wood with ball bearings and our go-cart was a fruit box on a plank of wood with wheels from a discarded pram. It was guided by string attached to the front wheel axle. The brakes were our feet and we wore out many a pair of boots in the process.

Some of the games we played are listed here. The streets were much safer then as there was much less traffic.

**Games without "equipment"** (other than pieces of chalk, wood or rag, stones, tin cans etc . . . )

*Hide and Seek*
One player was "on" in the "den". He or she closed their eyes and counted up to twenty, then shouted "Coming!" and tried to catch the other players, who had hidden themselves away. They tried to get "home" to the den without being seen. If seen or caught, they were "on" in turn.

*One Roll Two Roll* or *Sailor Boy Boy*
This was another hide and seek game. One would stand facing the wall and call "One Roll, Two Roll, Sailor Boy, Boy, Boy". At the end all would scatter to hide.

*Tin Can Copper*
The tin can was placed in the middle of the road. One child would stand by it with their eyes shut and count ten. The rest would run away and hide. When he or she opened their eyes, s/he would call out the places s/he thought the others were hiding, banging the can on the ground as s/he did so.

*Release*
For this game we split up into two teams, the cops and the robbers. We then drew a large box with a piece of chalk and the teams took turns in being cops and robbers. The robbers would run away and the chase would begin. To arrest a

71

robber you had to wrench his hands from his head and tap it three times before you could escort him to the box which was guarded by one of the cops. Being guard was the hardest job, because if one of the robbers who had evaded arrest got into the box and shouted "Release!" the robbers in the box would escape and have to be captured again. This was our favourite game.

## Fox and Sheep or Wolf
One player was the fox. The others lined up facing them, one behind the other and holding each other by the waist. The front player was the shepherd and tried to protect their flock against the fox, who tried to dodge behind and catch a sheep. The sheep, if caught, became the fox.

## Blind Man's Buff
One player was blindfolded and turned round several times to confuse them. The "Blind Man" then tried to catch someone, who, if caught, was "on" in turn.

## Hopscotch
Hopscotch was a game that was enjoyed by both boys and girls; it only required a piece of chalk and a stone. A large square was drawn and divided into eight smaller squares, each marked with a number. The stone was thrown into the first number. You hopped on one leg, picked it up and proceeded to the next number. If the other leg went to the ground you started from the beginning.

## Hey Jimmy Knacker
One boy would stand with his back to the wall as a buffer supporting about three other lads in a leapfrog position. Another team would then leap over the bending boys one at a time. Before leaping you yelled a warning call of "Hey Jimmy Knacker!"

## Carthorses
We would join hands behind our backs and gallop along the road like carthorses.

## Shoulder Charging
You had to hop around on one foot and charge your partner, who was doing the same, until one of you was knocked off balance.

## Head and Tails
It was played outside a sweetshop. You took it in turns to play. The leader would ask you to guess the name of the sweet. Raspberry Cream ("R.C." or Acid Tablet ("A.T."). In those days the window display would be very varied.

## Up the Wall

This was handstands with your feet resting against the wall.

## Statues

Two players (I think usually girls) joined their right hands and twirled each other round. When they stopped they had to take up a pose and become a statue. The rest tried to guess who or what it was.

## Winter Warmers

You obtained a can and punched several holes in it. Then you placed a piece of rag inside the can and set fire to it. The can was attached to a long piece of string, so you could swing it round and round.

Another game we played with tin cans was walking on them. They were attached to lengths of string, which we held in both hands to keep them steady.

## Tip-it

You needed two pieces of wood, one about twelve inches, the other about six inches long; two chalk rings drawn in front of the pavement kerb in the road; and two teams of as many as you had. You decided who was to "bat": the other side fielded. The "batsman" placed the shorter piece of wood on the edge of the kerb, overlapping, and whacked down on the part sticking out; the smaller piece flew up and forward and the batsman counted the number of taps from one of the chalk circles to the other. The batsman was "out" when the short piece of wood was

73

*Tip-it*

caught by a fielder. This went on until all the batsmen were out; then the other side batted. It was a dangerous game unless all the players had quick eyesight and quick movement – that short stick could really move sometimes.

*Cherry Hogs*
These were dried cherry stones which we would flick into a tin can or a cardboard box with a hole cut into it. Another game was to flick them at a screw stood on its head.

**Games with things**

*Marbles*
Marbles was played along the line of the kerb at the gutter. There were no set rules for marbles; they varied from group to group. The marbles themselves were coloured and made from hard glass. The one to start rolled a marble along the gutter; then if your opponent managed to hit it with his marble, he claimed a take; if it fell short, he would try and span the distance with his thumb and fore-finger. A boy with big hands had an advantage, so it was all very unsatisfactory - but a great game nevertheless.

74

*Ally Gobs* or its more genteel name *Five Stones*
It was four coloured stones with a largish coloured marble as a bouncer. It was a game for four, sitting comfortably on the kerbstone.

*Tops*
Not for us just the whip top that only kept the top spinning; we wanted ACTION! Here are two variations on ordinary tops.
*Peg Top:* These were about two inches in diameter. We would sharpen the peg on which they spun. Two, three or four boys would play this game. One would throw his top down – we perfected a way of throwing down a top wound in its string, so that it turned over and spun very fast. While the first boy's top was spinning on the pavement, the other boys would throw down their tops in the same way, trying to hit the spinning top in such a way that their sharpened peg would split it. Your top would be graded on how many matches it had survived. You could buy smaller boxwood tops; these were more expensive, but harder and more difficult to hit.
*Skimmer Tops:* These were flat topped; they were kept revolving by whipping with a short length of leather, lace or string. We had whips with a much longer string and by keeping the frayed end of the whip wet and learning how to strike the top in a certain way, we could make it travel though the air for some distance. Unfortunately many windows were broken in this way and there was the fear of hitting someone.

*Tops*

*Hoops*

There were hoops for girls and boys, which originally were identical, but later the boys acquired a pattern of their own. The introduction of the hoop as a plaything originated by using the hoops that secured barrels. Only the centre, top and bottom hoops could be used, as others had the contour of the barrel. Manufacturers soon saw the gain of producing hoops for children as a toy, which became part of the Christmas present. Incidentally the Hula-Hoop, used around the waist, a craze of the forties and fifties, was executed by young girls before the turn of the century.

Boys started using iron hoops; these travelled faster and by scrounging a meat-hook from the butcher to use as a "skimmer", one could "skim" the hoop along by hooking the hook around the iron hoop and pushing; this gave complete control for turning etc. Again the manufacturers soon began producing iron hoops with skimmers; some skimmers even had wooden handles. The local blacksmith was the right man to repair your broken iron hoop.

*Skipping*

Skipping was a pastime mostly enjoyed by girls. They would usually skip alone with a small piece of rope. Very often in the small narrow streets where we lived, mothers would help with a long rope – standing at each end and twirling it around; there could sometimes be as many as six girls jumping up and down. As the rope went over their heads and under their feet, they would chant little "Skipping Jingles" like:

"Salt, Mustard, Vinegar, Pepper";

"Green grass high, Green grass low,
All the boys will love you so,
Which one will it be,
Will it be the one for me?"

One for group skipping was:

"All in together this frosty weather
I spy Peter hanging out the window
SHOOT! BANG! FIRE!"
(at this the last one to leave the skipping rope in which all were skipping had to take over one end of the skipping rope).

One more for solo skipping was:

"Ebakanezer the King of the Jews
Bought his wife a pair of shoes
When the shoes began to wear
Ebakanezer began to S-W-E-A-R!"
(on these last five letters you had to jump as high as you could).

76

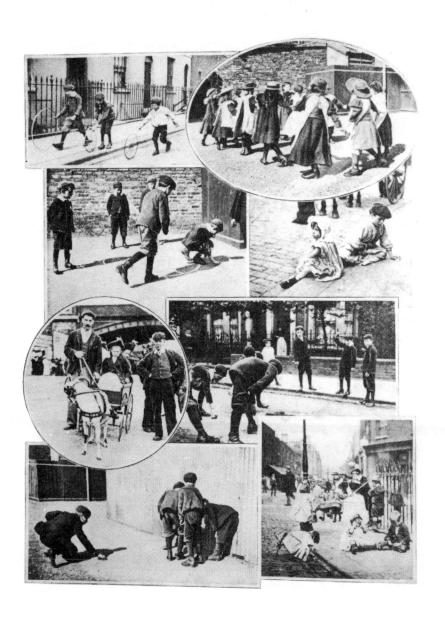

*Children's games*

## Yo-Yo

This game was to reach epidemic proportions with experts giving demonstrations in the large stores and on the stage of local cinemas, which ran competitions. A yo-yo was made of wood and perfectly balanced; the experts could almost make them talk. The yo-yo obtainable today is a very poor imitation.

## Bombs

After the First World War, a penny toy was produced of two halves (top and bottom) in the shape of a bomb; it was made of metal shaped as a bomb of the type that were dropped from aircraft by hand. The two halves were secured by a slip-knot loop of string. One could separate the two halves, place a "cap" (a small piece of paper with a touch of explosive on it) inside, pull the two halves together and throw the whole thing into the air. It would fall with the heavier end down and explode on hitting the ground. We later found we could attach a handkerchief by tying each corner to the string around the bomb, so that it would glide as a parachute to the ground before exploding.

## Cigarette Cards

I still get the urge to pick up discarded cigarette packets. It goes back to the time when as a child I hoped to find that the picture cards were still inside. We called them "Fag Cards".

One of the games we played with them was to stand one against the wall and try to knock it down by flicking other cards at it.

Another game was to flick them until one card landed on another.

## Halfpenny on the Line

For this game a line was drawn with a piece of chalk, at which we threw our halfpennies. The nearest to the line was the winner.

## Ball games

### Cannon also known as Cricket or Sticks

Four sticks were placed against the wall in the shape of a wicket; then you threw a ball at them. If you knocked them all down, you had to put them back into position again before somebody retrieved the ball and hit you with it.

### Queenie

The one with the ball stood with his back to the others; s/he would then throw it over their head. S/he could not turn round until somebody called out "QUEENIE!" S/he would then have to guess who had caught the ball.

### Throwing Balls at a Wall

You threw the ball against the wall, clapped once and caught the ball; then you did it twice and so on, as many claps as you could manage; or you could clap once

78

in front and once behind; or throw the ball, turn round and catch it. You were "out" when you dropped the ball.

## Wall Tennis

A line was drawn as high as three feet along a wall and this game could be played by two or four. A ball was bounced in front of the line so that it touched the wall above the drawn line; the opponent had to catch the ball, then bounce it in the same way. Spin could be put on a ball before throwing, which made it shoot off at an angle and made it difficult to catch. Points were scored when you made your opponent drop the ball. This game was also known as "The Wall Game" and was said to have been invented at Eton College in a space beside the Chapel.

## Nuisance Games

### Knock Down Ginger

This was basically just knocking on doors and running away. A variation was as follows, since most houses had doors close to each other. You tied one door knocker to the other next door with a piece of string which had enough slack so that when the door of one house was opened the knocker of the next door was raised ready for knocking. You knocked on the first door and hid opposite. The door was opened – no one there; the door was closed, so that the knocker next door fell and they opened their door – no one there; this would close the door and the next knocker fell. The opening of the doors became quicker each time. The game ended when you hid behind your own door, tossed a stone outside and watched the neighbours try to open their doors together.

### Window Tapping

A button was tied on to a short piece of black thread with a pin at the other end; you also had another long length of black thread, long enough to reach across the road. The pin was pressed into the wooden centre strut of the window, with the button hanging down. You returned to your hiding place behind the copeling on the other side of the road and pulled the thread, thus tapping the window with the button. The people would come out to see who was tapping on their window; their speed on coming out of the house would increase at each attempt to catch the tapper. Sometimes the people in the house at which you were hiding saw you, crept out and boxed your ears.

### Penny on the Pavement

You drilled a hole in a penny (the old pennies were much larger than the new), fixed a length of thread to the hole, hid behind the copeling and waited for someone to see the penny and try to pick it up; then you drew it away from them. If they had been caught before, they put their foot on the penny – then you'd had it.

# The Canal Mob
## Stan Hall (b. 1910)

It was in 1917, my eighth year, that I got to know the Canal Mob. Most of them lived in Neate Street, Camberwell, right on the bank. They were 85% of my class at school and what they lacked in finesse they made up in courage, loyalty and cheerfulness, making the best of the little that life had dealt them. Most, by this stage of World War I, were without fathers or, in some cases, brothers too. They had grown up fast to fill the gap in the family, to learn things they were not taught in school, for survival; and survive they did; there was no setback they could not surmount.

As for me, my father had been called up and my brother had already been killed. My mother had had to find a job in the bookbinding factory at the back of our house. Of my two sisters, one had left home already and the other was out at work making ammunition boxes. I was left largely to my own amusements. Every boy played in the street – there was nowhere else. So I went around to meet my schoolmates around the canal. This was great fun. There were barges tied up and others proceeding either up or down the canal. We could clamber from barge to barge and take rides on moving barges. Those drawn by horse we would offer to lead; better still, we would ride the horse. We were, of course, masters of the "dare" game, walking under the horse's tummy. We did this often in the main roads as well.

The whiting factories by the canal were supplied by barge and we would get a ride on an empty barge that was returning from delivering its load. We would wait at the Wells Way bridge knowing that the barge could not pass under at high water as this bridge was a low one. At a signal from the bargee, we would leap on to the barge to weigh it down in the water. We would then help to push the barge under the bridge by pushing with our feet and hands on the underside of the bridge. Those that didn't fall into the canal would ride as far as the Trafalgar Bridge, getting off there, returning home at the end of the day all without the knowledge of our mothers, we hoped. Of course I would deny any activity on or near the canal, even with the whiting and muck and dirt I had collected under the bridge, only to receive one of a great number of lectures from my mother about the dangers of the canal and "those horrible kids that live there." A lecture was not always the finish of the incident; sometimes physical efforts were used. I was lucky my parents were not the type that used force much, my father never. My mother, being Welsh, was more inclined to take a swipe in her anger. To keep out of distance for a few minutes usually resulted in her temper abating.

The other major pastime along the canal was swimming. Both sexes used the canal and as there were many unemployed, the ages could be up to sixteen years of age. The only person you had to look out for was the "Bobby". He would make regular patrols but his patrol time was known by all. Sometimes he would change

*The Canal Mob*

it. In that case, there was always the cottages, where the owner's children and his friends could leave their clothes and take refuge at the first sign of the "Bobby". Visitors to the canal would place their clothes in hidy holes and on the alert take refuge in the cottages. The "Bobby" couldn't come into the cottages, so he would wait around whilst the naked bodies hid inside. We never had Biology lessons at school; in fact we didn't even know it was called that, but the canal supplied the knowledge which was missed at school.

Our "mob" never ventured often along the cutting of the canal to Peckham, although it was only just the other side of the Trafalgar Bridge. The canal bank towards Peckham had the same layout of small houses backing on to the bank as Neate Street, a few little cottages, like Canal Place. The canal bank to Peckham was called Boathouse Walk, passing under the Commercial Road Bridge, one of two on the Peckham Branch. The other was Willowbrook Bridge (it changed its name to Bonar Road). This led to the High Street of Peckham. Here we found the Omnibus and Haulage Company of Thomas Tilling, who produced a petrol-electric bus that started off smoothly without a jerk; other buses nearly threw one out the back on starting. Tilling's depot was built over what was once a Bull Yard. It still retains the name Bull Yard today.

*A Tilling bus*

Our "territory" along our bank extended from the Camberwell Road to the Old Kent Road, where the canal disappeared under the Old Kent Road Bridge and continued on to Bermondsey and Rotherhithe. In that area there were even tougher breeds than Canal Place, Peckham; if possible, you could say they lived in even worse conditions. In those days the boys from each district stayed in their "patch"; a visit to the Bermondsey area was looking for a fight. It would not be long before we were running from the fray as their reinforcements gathered and outnumbered us. Their arrival would be received in the same way, should they pay a visit to Camberwell.

My membership of the "Canal Mob" lasted until I was well into my thirteenth year, although my attendance became less as I found other interests which the "mob" could not follow because they cost money and were above the basic ways of life. I was being given opportunities they would never receive.

My home was a couple of turnings north of Neate Street so I did not see "the mob" unless I went to their area. I missed the amusements invented from the barest things; children today do not have to make do with rubbish to invent.

The "mob" had taught me many things to add to my experience of life; they taught me loyalty to each other, basic but strong; satisfaction – they had to be satisfied with their lot; they taught me not to have fear and many other things. I am richer for knowing them; above all they taught me that possessions added nothing to your character.

## Streetraker
## Harry Hawes

I was a "Streetraker". On school holidays while Dad was at work as a dealporter at Surrey Docks (or in the pub) and Mum followed her employment as a waitress at "Ye Olde Coffee Shoppe" in Parkers Row, my pals and I lived it up.

We jumped on the backs of horse-driven carts until somebody called out to the driver, "Whip behind guv'nor!" Buses provided another game for us, leaping on the platform and jumping off again when spotted by the conductor.

Travelling on the tube was one of our pastimes. We would purchase a ticket for the cheapest fare (I think it was a penny) and journey miles around the network before getting off at the ticket's destination.

In spite of our parents' warnings, we just could not keep away from the riverside at Shad Thames and Horselydown.

One day my friend Georgie Bunclark had to be pulled out of the murky waters. I was blamed for pushing him.

There were lots of parks in Bermondsey. It was in Pussy Park, Long Lane, that Lennie Bunclark (Georgie's brother) was knocked out by the American see-saw and carted off in an ambulance. Again, I was blamed for taking him there.

In Coxons Park, Bill Borey broke his arm by falling off the slide.

The covered slide in St. James Park was a big attraction, as was the motorboat in Southwark Park where you could ride around the lake for a penny.

The recreation grounds in Tanner Street and Tooley Street were favourite playgrounds of ours.

In Tower Bridge Road was Bermondsey Park, and further down going towards Tooley Street was St. John's Park, in which stood St. John's Church, known locally as the lousy church, as the weathervane was reputed to be a louse. St. John's Church never survived the 1939-45 war. We were a big headache to the poor old park keepers who were always pleased when we moved on. I was eventually banned from Coxons Park!

Often we would cross over Tower Bridge to play with the cannons in the Tower and watch boats from all over the world coming to what was then the largest port in the world.

In the evenings I used to play nearer home – outside the India Arms public house on the corner of Boss Street and opposite the loading bay of Courage's brewery.

My reason for being there, like the children I played with, was that our parents were inside the pub drinking. This was a common occurrence in the thirties, when babysitters were unheard of. Not that we minded; it allowed us to stay up late.

Lemonade and crisps would come out from time to time to keep us quiet. If they did not children would stand at the pub door yelling for attention. Many a poor kid got a hefty clout for doing just that. Some parents thought more of their beery pals than their children.

Once a year the pub had an outing to the seaside and the men would be off in a char-a-banc loaded with beer. The children were there to see them off and as the coach pulled away we would shout: "Throw out yer 'mouldies' ". As the shower of coppers descended on us we would all dive to pick up as many as we could. Many a punch-up ensued in the scramble. When the men returned home we looked forward to the sticks of rock they brought back for us and when Dad was full of beer it was easy to tap him for extra pocket money.

Dad had a favourite lamp-post he used to hang on to after consuming too much ale and would wait for a friendly policeman to bring him home. He knew most of them as the pub was just a walk away from the station. Unfortunately one night a new copper to the district found him and put him in the cells for the night.

Another time when he never returned home from "The Indy", Mum had to go round and pull him out of the after-hours card school.

To get to our home you had to go down some steps and on one of our journeys to find Dad we found him flat on his face covered in snow where he had fallen down them. My sister Ivy and her friend Rosie Bunclark had earlier been jumping off the steps on to this lump of snow, not knowing it was our Dad.

The India Arms and Dad may not be with us any more, but memories of those days will remain with me forever.

# In the Workhouse
## Ada Bennett (b.1901)

My first recollection is of my father taking me into a pub and sitting me on the counter. I would sing and his mates would give me pennies. That was before my mother died. I was born in Chatham Street, Walworth, and was three years old when my mother died. I had a brother, who was five years old, and a sister, ten months old. Friends of the family took my sister and brought her up as their own. I did not meet her again until I was twenty. My father's aunt took my brother and me home with her, but could not keep us for long as she had ten children of her own. What happened to our home I do not know, so we ended up in the workhouse on and off for the next eight years.

When my father was working, he would have us home. Home was a furnished room with our coats on the bed for warmth, but we enjoyed those get-togethers. We would visit my father's aunt and play with her children, swinging on the lamp-posts, skipping in the street, whipping top or hoop and stick and visiting Kennington Park. When we got back my father would make all the children line up. He would play the piano and we would all do our party piece. It was great fun. Also my father would take us to the South London Palace in London Road on a Saturday evening. It cost sixpence for my father and threepence each for my brother and me. During the week my brother and I would wait outside the South London and ask people coming out of the first house for their programmes. Then we would sell them for a halfpenny to people going in the second house. In this way we were able to buy a ½d of fish or ½d of chips for our suppers. Sometimes I would clean neighbours' steps or mind a baby for a few coppers to help out.

My father was a painter and decorator and was very often out of work, more so in the winter. I remember one day when we were turned out of our room because we could not pay the rent. My father had threepence in his pocket. With that he bought some chips and we sat in the park to eat them. When the park closed we had nowhere to go, so we just walked about until after midnight and finished up in Westmorland Road Workhouse.

Let me tell you what it was like to go into the workhouse. First we were bathed and, as it was night time, put to bed in a nice clean bed with real blankets. Next day we were taken to four small houses round the corner in Boyson Road. My brother was in one house and I in another. I remember we were in the cottages (that is what we called them). It was in the year of George V's coronation and we were at dinner when we were told that the Southwark Guardians had sent tickets for some of us to see it from the stands in the Mall. We were given a lunch box. Also in our party were some children from Hanwell School near Harrow (that is the school we were sent to from the cottages). The coronation was something I shall never forget. Later I found that my future husband had been there as well, as one of the children from Hanwell School.

We lived in the cottages for a few weeks and were then taken to Hanwell by one of the House Mothers. We were housed in a separate block and isolated for three weeks. We were then taken to the main building. The boys were separated from the girls and would meet once a week when we had sport on the fields, weather permitting.

Our day started at 6 a.m. A boy would wake us up with reveille. Then it was to work. We all had our jobs to do; some polished dormitory floors; others cleaned toilets etc. All work had to be finished by eight o'clock. Then it was wash, clean our boots, do our hair, which was cut short like a boy's; then it was inspection by one of the nurses.

We had three nurses to each block and there were three blocks for the boys, two blocks for girls and one for babies; some of the girls were sent to help feed and change the babies. I was doing that when I was nine years old.

Breakfast was at 8.30, dinner 12.30, tea 5.00 and bed at 6.30 in the summer or 6.00 in winter. We did not attend school on Wednesday afternoon, but we did go on Saturday mornings. On Wednesday afternoons about ten of us girls would have to go to our dormitory with a nurse to sew buttons on or to mend or darn socks. Sometimes nurse would give us an old sheet and we would make rag dolls from it. Also Frank, my future husband, told me that if any of the boys were given an old sheet they would tear it into strips and wind it round a small stone; in that way they made a hard ball for cricket. We would get our needle and cotton from our head nurse.

To each dormitory we had a "Corporal" and "Sergeant". They were the older girls. They were also in charge at meal times. If anyone wet their bed, they would have to stand on the form to eat their meals for the day and help to make the beds in their dormitory. When we got up in the morning we had to show our sheets to the nurse; if they were all right we would help each other to fold them and our blankets; we would put them on top of each other with all colour strips in line; then we would wrap our quilt around the lot and put them on the pillow, ready to be made up in the afternoon by the girls who had wet their beds or by the nurses.

But the school was not all hard discipline. It was our own school and had a swimming pool, infirmary, sports ground and a band; also it was nearly self-supporting, with our own farm, kitchen garden, laundry and cook house. The older boys and girls used to help after school in these places. We were given sixpence each on New Year's Day and our head nurse would keep account of it in a book and each time we went out for a walk with one of the young nurses we would be given a penny to buy sweets. However, my brother could not bear to be closed in. He ran away about three times. Once he walked all the way from Harrow to my father's aunt's at Kennington and when he was returned to school he was given the birch. It did not make him bitter; in fact it was the opposite – he became a very kind man, ready to help anyone, and was very grateful for the way the school had looked after us. I left the school for the last time when I was nearly twelve years old, because my father had met a woman whom he married – and that is another story.

## Life in a Flat
## Edith Carpenter (b. 1918)

We did not live in a house, but a small flat. The property belonged to the Southern Railway. It was similar to the Guinness Flats so much talked of today. We had an inside lavatory and a scullery, with sink and cold tap. But unlike many families of that age, we were self-contained. Once we closed our door, we had no contact with our neighbours at all.

We slept two in a bed and it was just normal practice; we knew no different. The scullery contained a coal box, a gas cooker and a copper. The copper used to boil the washing and had to be lit with wood and paper. Coal was the fuel used, for both the copper and the fires in the other rooms. The copper was also lit on Fridays to supply us with the vast amount of water we needed for our weekly baths.

Another item of furniture in the scullery was a large wringer. This was an absolute necessity, for the washing had to be dried indoors, unless you felt energetic enough to walk up to the roof, five floors up, where it could be hung among the smoking chimneys of the ten flats below, for there were two flats to each landing and we lived on the ground floor.

Washing in those days meant pre-wash for whites, boiling in the copper, rinsing and then finally dipping in the "blue water" made by a small linen bag containing a blue substance; the name of this product was Reckitts. The Reckitts blue bag made the whites look whiter. I can hear you all saying, "Why not Daz?" But the only soap powder in those early days of my life was Hudson, bought in small packets (about 1½d. per packet). The ordinary soap was Sunlight. A scrubbing board and small scrubbing brush were used to loosen the dirt from soiled garments.

As for bath soap, first it was White Windsor, bought by the piece and cut up in the shop; then it was Family Health, a torrid smelling soap, coloured red; it went slimy if it was left in the water too long. My mother used to try to keep the soap to harden, for it lasted longer then. Later, much later, it was Knight's Castile toilet soap we were to use. This was a product of the makers of Family Health soap, Knight's, and it had a faint perfume; it was white, as it is today.

The only bath salts were the soda we put in to soften the water; good old-fashioned soda, so little used today, yet it was used for everything in my youth.

We had never heard of washing-up liquid, nor did we have scouring powder to clean the cutlery. We had steel cutlery, not stainless as used today, and it needed cleaning after each meal. The abrasive used was Monkey Brand, a block of hardened material, something like pumice stone soap is today. The gas cooker was fitted in the flat; there were no fancy ones in those days; they were all black and free to the user. Later it became the thing to rent a better type, black and white, for about 3d. per week. It sounds very cheap, but remember, the man's wage, if he was lucky enough to have work, was about 35 shillings a week and there were usually many children, for whom no family allowance or assistance was available. Rent was about ten shillings for our flat, paid weekly of course.

We lived on plain wholesome food, bread and jam or syrup; margarine was used, not butter; that was kept to be eaten on its own – best butter, as we called it. The bread was not cut and wrapped as today's cardboard, but bought from the baker's, hot from the oven and weighed to reach the two pounds it was supposed to weigh; a slice or two were added to make the weight up. Bread was seldom eaten hot, for it would go further when a little stale.

Nothing was wasted in our house. Bread puddings were made with the week's leavings of bread. Shops sold cakes as cheaply as two for a penny, but my mother baked an amount, kept them in a tin and they lasted us the whole week, one a day each, with our tea; rock cakes they were called, but don't get me wrong – they were not hard at all.

She shopped weekly whenever possible, buying her stores at Coppen's in the Lambeth Walk; her cheese and margarine, eggs and bacon, at Dean's, another shop in the Walk. Vegetables were bought from a stall in the Lower Marsh. Meat (there were no fridges in those days) was bought daily. I often went to the butchers, Wilson's in the Lower Marsh, before I went to school; it would be 1 lb. of stewing steak for a meat pie, 1 lb. of leg of beef for a meat pudding, scrag end of lamb for a stew or 1½ lb. of beef sausages for a toad-in-the-hole. I never bought the weekend joint, which was usually beef and served us for Monday, washday, cold with Bubble and Squeak and pickles, with a rice pudding to fill us up. It was called Bubble and Squeak, I always believed, from the way it squeaked when being fried in the fat, for it was usually the excess cabbage and potatoes from the Sunday's cooking. The bacon bought at the weekend would be used for a rolypoly; that was tasty too. There were none of your convenience foods in those days; I think we had more nourishing and tasty food then. Some Saturdays we had pie and mash from Harris's, the pie shop in the New Cut; the price was twopence for the pies and one penny for the mash and liquor. When we were older, we used to sit in the pie shop on our own and eat them in the shop.

My mother made almost all our clothes, taking clubs for our shoes. Some neighbour would run a club, a shilling a week a share for twenty weeks; each participant would pick a number and every week someone would have a pound to spend at Jackman's, a shoe shop in Drury Lane (it still exists). We were all treated the same; my mother would take all four of us to Jackman's; their shoes were about five shillings a pair, school-type, so that they would last longer. We did have the patent type shoe when they became fashionable, but only for Sundays; they were not strong enough for everyday wear.

As time went on, my elder sister Cissie went to work and Mum felt we were able to care for ourselves a bit; so she got a job in the Treasury office, cleaning. She left home at 6.00 am, coming back at 10.00 am and returned to work at 5.30, arriving back at eight o'clock. She walked over Westminster Bridge morning and night. I had the task of getting the others up, for I always woke early. Mum would give me a cup of tea in bed and I would then get up and wake the rest of the girls later. I liked the peace of the early mornings and even now I still get up early. In those days, I would go to the butcher's and the baker's before I went to school. On Mondays, I would light the copper, after filling it with cold water, so that it would be boiling for Mum to start her washing when she came home from work. She would leave the porridge cooking in the steamer for us and as she was there for our midday meal and our 4.30 homecoming for our tea, we did not suffer from neglect by her working.

My mother still attended to the housework; our only daily job was the tea things, washing them up and putting on the best tablecloth, the green plush tasselled one; this covered over the oilcloth one we used for meals and changed the room completely, making it look more of a "best room" than a kitchen.

One other chore we got was the weekly shopping; this was not really a chore, but an adventure: watching the weighing up of the various goods, having the perks of the "makeweight" of the piece of cheese that was always added to the purchase, just as we had the additional slice of bread, bought from the baker's; besides, shops would often give a child a taste of something, while serving.

The list prepared by my mother for the groceries was soon abandoned, for it was so regular that we knew it by heart. One luxury we had been enjoying for some time was cheesecakes, bought at Coppen's for the price of five for sixpence; they were huge fluffy things that made a right old mess when eaten, with icing sugar coating, festooned with coconut strips. We got used to having these as a treat on Fridays with our tea. Having five meant that for once my mother could have one too. Then we saw cream horns. "Can we get cream horns, instead of cheesecakes?" we asked. "Yes, if you all want them", my mother replied. Now we tasted cream horns; the cream would go right down to the tip if you pushed it with your tongue – they were grand.

We not only enjoyed our shopping, but also watching other people doing theirs, for the shopkeepers would not rush any purchaser and anything asked for was, if humanly possible, obtained. Does anyone remember the Jewish clothes shops? You dared not pause to look in the window, for a woman would emerge from nowhere and entice you to "Just try it on, dear – or why not come in and look – you don't have to buy" or "You can have it saved for a deposit of a shilling."

89

One of these shops in the Lower Marsh, called Segal's, specialised in mourning clothes, the hideous fashion of even the poor to go into all black clothes for funerals and a period of mourning: twelve months for the nearest and dearest, six months for sons and daughters, three months for grandchildren. Being in mourning meant everything, even stockings. Clothes were dyed black and the custom was rigidly adhered to. When my grandfather died in 1925, we children were all dressed in black; our cotton summer dresses were dyed and we were subjected to the tastelessness for three months that summer. One of our aunts always bought a black coat, for as I have often heard her say, "I would like to have bought a new brown coat, but someone is sure to die if I do and then it will have to be dyed black." Recalling this, we must realise, that with the size of families and their closeness of contact, it was a continual process of someone dying in the family. When my brother died in 1931, we had six months of mourning. Fortunately they were mainly winter months.

His death meant that a move was no longer necessary, so we continued to live in the flat we had been born in. We had acquired a dog and a parrot, the latter from a grateful neighbour; he was a sailor. My mother as usual stood in as a midwife to help his wife, taking care of his children while his wife was confined to her bed for the then usual fortnight. My mother was the local social worker, I feel, always ready to help the needy, even if she herself had not got much. The women of those days were so very poor that when they were giving birth they had no proper medical attention, for that meant paying a doctor's bill. Even the midwife charged for her help; my mother had once completed a course of first aid, so everyone assumed she was as good as a nurse. She often brought poor kids, whose mother was in bed, home to sit at our table and eat; many's the time her own meal I feel. She would be called on to bandage a badly cut knee or to lance a boil; "boils" were very prevelant in those days, probably due to bad diet.

On the lighter side, in those days all families had a get-together, for there was no television or radio to entertain the masses; they made their own amusement. My husband's family, the Carpenters, met at their shop on Saturdays, all the relatives and their children. My husband Charlie often told me of the antics the children would get up to, left to their own amusement, roaming through Lambeth Walk to spend the pennies their uncles had given them.

First stop would be the pie shop, for faggot and pease pudding; then it would be the fish shops for a pennyworth of crackling (crackling being the batter that had parted from the fish while being cooked). The next stop was the baker's for a lump of bread pudding, then the sweet shop. How they weren't all sick beats me.

After the shop had closed and the stall been taken in, the eats would begin in earnest and the drink would flow. The songs would be yodelled and everyone had their own party piece.

*The Elephant and Castle*

Festivities ending well after midnight, it meant walking home, for the trams never ran after twelve o'clock on Saturdays in those days.

Charlie's two aunts, who lived in the Old Kent Road area with their families, would accompany his family travelling the same way. First through China Walk, along Lambeth Road, past the site on which the War Museum now stands. One of the uncles would say, "Let's get rid of these kids, put them in Bedlam." The children would run for their lives, in terror, yet knowing that it would not happen. This was because the site on which the Imperial War Museum now stands was in those days a private nursing home for mental patients. It still has those high iron railings and the heavy iron gates; in those days it also had a green wooden door with a brass pull-type bell. The brass plate at its side said "Please ring" and not many children (or adults!) in my day could refuse the invitation to ring. Children love to be scared.

Charlie's uncle would pull the bell; no one ever came to answer it, but it got the children moving faster, for they would almost be to the Elephant and Castle by the time the adults started walking again.

Up the St. George's Road they would go, turning at the Elephant and Castle into the Walworth Road, right through Walworth Road, (as it was until it changed its name to Camberwell Road) to Albany Road, a short distance past the Camberwell Gate. Still they weren't home, for they had to walk half way down Albany Road too. At Albany Road the relatives would say their goodbyes and plod on the rest of their way home.

*One Tree Hill*

*Surrey, 1914*

# Chapter 5
# Outings, Treats and Holidays

## Days Out
## Leslie Piper (b. 1908)

Most of my outings during the summer were spent on One Tree Hill. We walked of course; none of us had any money for fares. In fact, as I recall it, we had no money for anything. We took our food, usually bread and jam wrapped in newspaper, and a bottle which we could fill with water and add a couple of scented cashews to give it a hint of flavour – or at any rate a little colour so that we thought it tasted better – a kind of auto-suggestion probably.

We spent most of the day there, playing games and catching grasshoppers, with which the place abounded.

The Crystal Palace railway line ran by Brenchley Gardens and we used to cross the line on our way home. This was before the line was electrified.

A wonderful view can be obtained from the top of the hill and it is said that Queen Boadicea made a stand here against the Romans.

A more organised outing was with our Sunday School (at All Saints Church, just off Sumner Road) to Dog Kennel Hill.

The right side of Dog Kennel Hill as one ascends, which is now a housing estate, was once an extremely different kind of estate. The houses were large country houses with their own gardens. We travelled there by horse brake from Peckham. It was a great treat for us but, I fancy, would seem very tame to the children of today.

I think that our only day school outing in those days consisted of a day at Riddlesdown. We went by tram to Croydon and then changed to a Croydon tram to Purley, marching the rest of the way and, of course all the way back. All we had there was a glass of milk and a bun and there was little in the way of amusement beyond the grounds and a small zoo. Our pocket money was very limited and very soon exhausted, as we were ourselves.

We also went on outings connected with sport. My brother was four years older than me and so hardly of my generation, as four years seems a big difference when you are young. But he often took me out on Saturdays, sometimes to see cricket at the Oval. We would spend all day religiously marking the score card and working out the bowling analysis. These were the days of such Surrey stalwarts as Jack Hobbs, Andy Sandham, Bill Hitch and Herbert Strudwick and four or five hundred runs was quite common for a day's play.

Sometimes we would go to Herne Hill to watch London Welsh rugby team play although I confess I didn't understand the game; in fact I still don't.

We often went to Champion Hill to watch the amateur soccer club Dulwich Hamlet – then at the height of their career.

On one occasion my brother took me to a sports meeting at Stamford Bridge. Here I saw the great Jimmy Wilde box an exhibition bout with Joe Conn. His speed was amazing and his ability to avoid punishment a great asset that many modern boxers would do well to emulate.

A different kind of outing was to the cinema or the music hall.

Opposite the Lord Nelson public house in Old Kent Road there stands a building which in my childhood was the Nelson cinema. I used to be taken here when I was very small – too young to be interested in the films. I used to crawl under the seats in search of silver paper or any other 'valuables' that I might be lucky enough to find. Later there were many cinemas in Peckham – there were three in Rye Lane alone. The Imperial Playhouse stood somewhere about where Marks & Spencers is today and in the old silent days they had a lady violinist called Ruby Oth, as well as a pianist to accompany the films and to play solos during the interval. An attendant used to walk about spraying the air. Whether this was done as a disinfectant or as a deodorant I don't know – possibly a bit of both. My father used to display a poster in his blacksmith's shop in Melon Road advertising the programme for the Hippodrome in the High Street. This entitled us to two free circle tickets each week. My parents were not keen on pictures, so I used to take a friend with me. We loved to follow the serials. Tarzan, then played by Elmo Lincoln, and Houdini, the famous escapologist, were two of our favourites. We were always left at the most exciting and breathtaking point and had to wait another week to know how the hero or heroine cheated an almost certain death. Bags of peanuts were eaten as a very popular form of refreshment and the shells were dropped on the floor without compunction. They made quite a noise as people moved along to their seats and must have presented quite a problem to the cleaners, who I take it hadn't the benefit of the modern vacuum cleaner. The Hippodrome, formerly the Crown, was replaced by what is now the Top Rank Bingo Hall.

Later, when the big cinemas came along, they ran live shows during the interval; they provided first class entertainment. I remember seeing the Billy Cotton Band Show at the Trocadero at the Elephant and Castle and the Albert Sandler Trio at the Old Kent Road Astoria.

The films were a very popular form of entertainment, especially for courting couples, who appreciated the comforting darkness and seclusion of the back row, which enabled them to indulge in their amorous activities without embarrassment to themselves or to others who were more keen on watching the film. In this permissive age of course, couples would not be so self-conscious – or so considerate of other people's feelings!

*A music hall gallery*

The Music Hall was still flourishing in my youth; I was an ardent follower, usually at the New Cross Empire or the Camberwell Palace. Among the popular stars of that time were Gertie Gitana, G. H. Elliott, Harry Champion, Talbot O'Farrell and the very young Ted Ray with his "Fiddling and Fooling". Gertie Gitana was one of the first people I remember who played saxophone solos and the audience would never let her go until she sang their favourite "Nellie Dean", which she had made her own number. We thoroughly enjoyed these programmes, but looking back, I don't think that many of the artists would have made the grade today.

The National Sunday League used to promote Sunday afternoon concerts. these were very good; we saw some first class performers. The standard of production was strictly governed however; the artistes had to be in evening dress; and nothing offensive was permitted. The New Cross Empire ran a lot of these concerts and we had a long programme starting at about 3 p.m.

Lastly, I must mention one other form of entertainment – the melodrama at the Elephant and Castle theatre. Tod Slaughter was the hero in most of these spine chilling plays such as Sweeny Todd, Maria Martin and the Speckled Band, We loved them.

95

# Going to the Pictures
## Ben Moakes (b. 1904)

All those people who, like me, were born in the early years of this century have grown up with the cinema, reached their prime with the cinema and are now declining with the cinema.

The early films had just a novelty value and were shown wherever a suitable hall could be rented. Music halls would feature 'the bioscope' as an added attraction.

No film lasted more than half an hour and was usually accompanied by a piano tinkling out appropriate music.

We children had plenty of choice between cinemas that catered for youngsters. There was one in Walworth Road, near Liverpool Grove, and the hall that stands behind the Visionhire premises nearby was called 'The Electric' cinema. There was also 'The Gem' in Carter Street opposite the Beehive Public House.

My elder brother and I were given a penny each for our weekly visit to the pictures. We favoured the little cinema near Liverpool Grove.

The procedure was to buy a penny ticket each at the paybox outside; then, on entering, half the ticket would be taken by an usher, the other half being retained.

The seating consisted of rows of wooden forms. After two or three short films had been shown, the lights were switched on and the remaining half tickets were collected from us. The children who had arrived earlier and seen their full pennyworth would have to leave.

At the end of the next part of the programme once more the lights went on and we, having no ticket, would go out.

But my brother and I liked to have sweets to suck, so we spent a halfpenny on toffee before getting to the cinema, then bought one penny ticket and one halfpenny ticket. This meant that one of us, it was always me, had to leave after the first half was seen. So we planned a fiddle. I would lay full length under the form when the collector came, hidden by the legs of the other children. They also spread themselves along to cover the space I had occupied. As soon as the lights went out I climbed back on the form. But after a while they got wise to us. A man came in with a broom that had a long bamboo handle. "Hold up your feet", he shouted, then plunged the broom under the forms to detect anybody lying there.

Eventually Mum gave us an extra halfpenny for our sweets.

Eddie Polo was one of our early film heroes. He had fights in every picture, getting his shirt ripped each time.

Two of our cowboy heroes were William S. Hart and Broncho Billy Anderson. Tom Mix came later. Charles Ray was the college boy heart-throb for the girls.

In the many fights we saw on the screen, our heroes always fought fairly. When they had knocked down their antagonist, they stood back to allow him to get up. But the villains would frequently kick the man who was on the ground.

After a few years we got the serials, with an exciting episode every week, the hero or heroine being left in a desperate situation each time. From this the word 'cliff-hanger' evolved.

"The Shielding Shadow" was a serial that intrigued us with its trick camera effects showing only the hands of an invisible man who foiled the villains every time. We all knew that Jerry Carson was The Shielding Shadow. He couldn't be seen because he used a substance left in a jar by a scientist.

"The Exploits of Elaine", "The Hazards of Helen" and "The Perils of Pauline" were all serials and Pearl White was the blonde heroine who stole the hearts of growing lads – us!

Several years later, in the twenties, Pearl White cashed in on this by appearing in "The London Revue" at The Lyceum Theatre, receiving a fabulous sum for swinging on a rope across the stage. Incidentally, a young eccentric dancer dressed as a page boy also featured in the show. He was an 18 year old named Max Wall.

During the 20's and 30's new purpose-built cinemas sprang up and several music halls changed from live performances to films.

We who lived near Camberwell Green were well catered for. On Denmark Hill The Camberwell Palace and The Empire became cinemas, The Empire being rebuilt later and renamed The Odeon.

The present Post Office on Denmark Hill stands on the site of The Bijou. We pronounced it 'Bye-Joe'.

The Golden Domes was erected on the other side of the road. Here we saw films and heard live bands. I remember first hearing the song "Valencia" in 'The Domes'. The band leader jokingly told us we would have to learn to whistle the tune in Spanish. The International supermarket occupies the site now.

In Camberwell New Road, the "New Grand Hall" was built. I was a regular patron. Exploration films made by Mr. and Mrs. Martin Johnson held me spellbound as a teenager.

The Regal Cinema in Camberwell Road, now a bingo club, went up a lot later, just before the outbreak of war in 1939.

Between Boundary Lane and Boyson Road an early cinema was built, which for some reason we called "Jenkins". Here I attended the children's shows on Saturday mornings. I remember the large illuminated clock near the screen which bore the words "Sandows Cocoa" instead of numerals. This building is now Hammond's car saleroom.

The Montpelier, just off John Ruskin Street, (Beresford Street in those days), showed films as well as live entertainment.

In Arnside Street "The Purple Picture Palace" had a rather short life. Its place has been taken by the Post Office and other shops.

At the Elephant and Castle the Hyams Brothers built 'The Trocadero'. The great Sophie Tucker appeared on stage on the opening night in foggy December.

The Elephant Theatre opposite, home of "Sweeney Todd", also became a cinema.

Peckham had its share of newly-built cinemas. "The Tower" in Rye Lane was outstanding. There was also The Gaumont in Peckham High Street. When the war finished, in 1945, my daughter was a projectionist at The Tower. It was the custom for The Tower and The Gaumont to share the current news-reel, which was carried to and fro by the employees of each cinema. She became acquainted with a young ex-sailor projectionist of The Gaumont and they eventually married.

But let us go back to those years between the wars, when bigger and better palaces were built to compete for our patronage, each with its own style of architecture. The Granada at Tooting had a cathedral-like atmosphere; the Brixton Astoria's interior made us feel we were outdoors on a starry night in Spain; but the Old Kent Road Astoria was much more down-to-earth.

One last thing: all these super cinemas had Hammond or mighty Wurlitzer organs, which could produce the sounds of a full orchestra and a host of other noises. The resident organists became stars in their own right. Everybody listened to Quentin McLean at The Trocadero.

*"The Troc"*

# The Cinemas of Bermondsey
## Harry Hawes (b. 1922)

Louis Mordish played the organ,
the stage shows were a wow.
How I wish that I could go
into the *Trocette* now.

I remember going to the *Grand*,
when I was just a boy,
and seeing in The Desert Song
John Boles and Myrna Loy.

In a cinema called the O.K,
which was short for the *Old Kent*,
I went to see the first long film
and straight to sleep I went.

At the *Globe* in Old Kent Road,
each week I held my breath,
as vampire bats and monsters
scared me half to death.

To the *Elephant and Castle*
I went with my first date
we saw a film called Cyclops,
its "One Eye' thought was great.

The *Trocadero* cinema,
the plushest place in town,
had well known artists on the stage
and films of great renown.

As I lived in Fair Street,
I found it quite a walk,
when going to the cinema
to see films at the *Stork*.

Flicks at the *Rialto*,
then some pie and mash,
and still get change from one and six –
that's real value for cash.

The *Palace* down on Ambrose Street
was owned by Harry Share –
now gone but not forgotten,
by people who went there.

At the *Star* – our tuppenny rush –
the villains got the bird,
as noisy kids made such a din
you couldn't hear a word.

When at the *Astoria*
at "Bunking In" we played
by getting hold of ticket stubs
and saying we had paid.

"Take me in please mister",
you'd often hear us say,
if films were adult only
and youngsters turned away.

Goodbye old cinemas of my youth –
I'm sad you did not last,
your age of greatness ended,
your heyday too soon past.

# Music Halls and Theatres
## Alice Cordelia Davis (b. 1898)

South London had some very good Music Hall. The Camberwell Palace in Denmark Hill was a very popular one, the Camberwell Empire too, which was on the corner of Coldharbour Lane. The Empire in its earlier days had been a theatre. In the time I remember, it was used for music hall. My first visit was connected with "bath night". I'll tell you why. We did not have a bathroom, so our kitchen was used for bath night. As there was such a lot of us, my father was encouraged to go out for a few hours, which he did, to one of the music halls. As a special treat he would take me with him.

I loved going; it was like another world; and so it was – of make believe. The cost to go in was very low. The Empire was cheaper. We used to go in the "Pit"; that was the ground floor. Sometimes we would go in the "Early Doors"; that meant you paid a few coppers more to go in before the others waiting in the queue.

The Camberwell Palace was a better place; it also had first class artists. They were called "turns". I saw all the tip-top artists of that time. At weekends it was a job to get in; a notice board outside would say "House Full". Each artist would have their own songs and patter. Some used the same material for many years. They would perhaps go to two or three halls each evening. They all worked very

100

*Doorman, Camberwell Palace*

hard. The hard-working folk of South London always enjoyed their efforts. What I could never understand was why people had to have a "good cry" to prove they were enjoying themselves. I heard my mother say (she too used to go now and again) "There was not a dry eye in the house". You see, in between the singers and acrobats, a one-act play would be played and usually it was the sadder part of some well known play. A favourite part was the murder of Marie in "The Red Barn" or Bill Sykes and Nancy. Bill always had his dog, a flat-faced bulldog. The screams of Nancy were worth paying to go in the "Early Doors" for.

Another turn my father used to love to listen to was the solo violinist. My father would say, "He can make that fiddle speak".

As for theatres, the four I remember most were The Kennington Theatre, Deptford Theatre, The Crown and the Elephant Theatre. All in their times were very popular.

The Elephant, I believe, was the largest. The regulars came to enjoy themselves and they did. The actor I remember most was "Tod Slaughter" – he was always the hero. The company would put a new play on each week. Most were blood-thirsty, sometimes noisy. The company always had a dark-eyed villain with flashing eyes! Also a very wicked old man, sometimes a wicked old woman and always a young girl who suffered a lot. This was enjoyed by all. There was a long interval. Off the side of the stage was an exit door that led to a bar. The regular patrons would go into the bar and treat the actors. While this was going on, a young man would bring a large basket into the audience. The ladies would enjoy some pigs trotters and ham rolls while their gentlemen friends would bring in some bottled beer.

I used to like having a large arrowroot biscuit – it was as large as a small saucer; or perhaps a "pound cake" which was like a large fairy cake with currants in the top and a paper collar round it.

My father took me a few times – I loved every minute of it. The most enjoyable part to me was at the end of the show when the actors would walk across the stage to receive their applause, commencing with the lead, who would be clapped and whistled very loudly. When the villain took his turn the boos and whistles and hisses would be exciting to hear.

## Treats
## Lilian Blore (b. 1905)

One big treat was that after Christmas my father would take all the family to the pantomime at the Elephant and Castle Theatre. The theatre and all the Elephant and Castle have been rebuilt and many of the roads have been built across now.

A smaller treat was that every Friday evening, when my father came home from work with his wages, after his meal he would take all the family to the Montpelier cinema in Walworth. There was a film, news reel and after the film you would have a stage show, all for threepence for adults and tuppence for children.

I would also go out with my friend. Mondays we went to the Camberwell Palace of Varieties on Denmark Hill. On the stage we would see different actors and actresses every week – G. H. Elliott, Randolph Sutton, Marie Lloyd, Harry Lauder, Gertie Gitana, Florrie Ford, Nellie Wallace, Harry tate, "Little Tick" with the big boots, and many more. We paid fourpence to go in. The Camberwell Palace is now pulled down.

## Blackheath
## Harry Hawes (b. 1922)

Bank Holidays were the days when children took their sandwiches and pocket money (such as it was) and caught the tram from Tooley Street to Greenwich for the day.

Approaching the Heath there were kerbside traders with all sorts of goods for sale. Saucy hats, things to wave and goodies to eat and drink. Gaily coloured carts sold ice creams and hokey pokey and in the distance could be heard the magical sound of the fair. Although we never had enough money to go on all the rides and play all of the games, the atmosphere and the gaiety of the fairground activities aroused our feelings to fever pitch. At the end of the day we would return home tired but happy.

# We Made Our Own Fun
## Alice Cordelia Davis (b. 1898)

We made our own fun. My father played the mandolin – we children played any music and he would "follow" us.

On special occasions we would give a "musical evening". Our aunts and uncles would come, mostly on Saturday evening. Of course the uncles and aunts were not old, so they too enjoyed the musical evenings. As they all sat around the room each would be asked to sing a song. The aunts all sang sad songs. My mother said they were "ballads". One aunt was a tall pale-faced lady with large dark eyes. She would sing staring up to the ceiling. She had a high voice with a very pronounced trembling – it got worse as she got to the high notes at the end. I am sorry to say us children would have to go from the room; we would explode with laughter on the stairs.

The uncles all sang jolly songs and we all joined in the chorus. My father always sang "Away went Polly, with her Steps so Jolly". Yes, everyone had their own song. Our programme was varied. We would also play overtures to the operas. The "News of the World" published the popular songs of the day. The music and the serial that was also published was a good pennyworth. "Don't go Down in the Mine, Dad", "Blue Eyes, True Eyes", both were published, both joined our "rep", which would be fitted into a brown paper cover.


# Holidays
## Edith Carpenter (b. 1918)

Holidays were unheard of for working class families, but we children did have the introduction of two types of holiday at school. One was the School Journey, a semi-educational fortnight, spent during term-time, with two teachers. The areas we were taken to were usually the seaside, where there was access to many historical places and nature reserves. The other was the Country Holiday Fund, as we called it; that was two weeks spent at the home of country folk, strangers who opted to cater for London children, for a fee, during the summer holiday break. I went on both of these, for my mother tried not to deprive us of more than was absolutely necessary.

The first country holiday I spent was with my eldest sister, in 1926. We went to a village outside Bath and had a whale of a time. We were very fortunate to be placed with a family that not only owned a pony and trap, but would sometimes take us out in it with them. We left London on the first Thursday of the start of the summer holiday from school and arrived back on a Thursday two weeks later. The cost of the holiday was assessed according to the family's income, for it was

103

clearly subsidised by the London County Council, now known as the GLC. Some could be paying as much as a pound and others as little as five shillings for the whole holiday, including the fare. To whoever introduced this treat for the poor I give my heartfelt thanks.

On school journeys, the rate was a set one for all comers, usually 30 shillings for the fortnight; again this included the fares for the return journey and the many trips made during the fortnight – very reasonable.

The following year I went on a country holiday with my sister Rosie, while Cissie, my eldest sister, went to Seaford with the school journey. Although she had thoroughly enjoyed the previous year's holiday with me, the school journey really sent her into ecstasies. Never before had she been so carried away with the prospect of yet another one the following year. As soon as we returned to school after our summer break her name was down for the next year's journey and her sixpence a week being recorded to ensure she got a place, for this event only catered for thirty girls (thirty boys went with two masters at another time and place).

I went on a country holiday again early in the autumn term. I paid in my threepence per week towards it, the same as my sister.

I remember that year, Rosie and I stayed with a nice old couple and two of our London neighbour's family stayed with the neighbours of our 'country parents'. The local doctor, who had for some reason to visit our house every day, would take us four children for a ride in his car. We had never been in a car before that time. He would pack us all in and drive to the next patient. We would sit in the car hoping for another little trip when he came out. The local busy-body, who lived next door to this patient, would constantly tell us that we should not be in the doctor's car because we would do some damage. One day she must have been very pleased, for someone must have taken off the handbrake; the car being parked on a steep hill, started to gather momentum. We were all scared, especially when, at the bottom of the hill, the road curved round a sharp bend. But with more luck than judgement, we managed to stop, just avoiding a haystack. We jumped out and ran for dear life, not knowing whether we had damaged the car or not. The poor GP had to walk down the hill to recover his property. We kept out of his sight for a couple of days, but he caught up with us and enjoyed the tale of how scared we were, for he had a good laugh. I suppose looking back we were in not the slightest bit of danger, but then we thought we were going to suffer injury, if not death!

We assisted the local farmer with his harvesting until a girl from our school, also lodging in the village, stuck a pitchfork in another girl's neck. Fortunately it was not serious, but that was the end of our farming days. I dare say the farmer felt he would get on better without us and was in fear of more injuries to us nuisances.

The holiday came to an end all too soon and we were home again to enthrall our sisters and friend with our exploits. Back to school in late August and we started paying our threepence per week towards the next year's holiday, Cissie paying her

104

sixpence a week towards her school journey.

In 1929 I took Cissie's place on the School Journey. The trip was to the Isle of Wight and she was afraid of crossing the water, so I had a bonus holiday.

It was very different from the country holidays. We were housed in a large dormitory, the teachers having their own little rooms apart from us. We ate in a hall, were given packed lunches to take out with us and evening meal when we returned. We had coaches to pick us up most days and were taken to many places of interest, including Osborne House, Carisbrook Castle and the lighthouse. We could see the outside of Parkhouse Prison – it was not all that far from where we stayed at East Cowes. We had, unlike the other type of holiday, to show some of the educational advantages we had gained from the visit: we had to write essays, press leaves and flowers and keep a diary of our visits.

# Hopping
## Tom Ash (b. 1927)
### *Extract from Tom's own book 'Childhood Days'*

The season we liked best was in September. This was the hop-picking season and it was at this time of year that most of us in the area we lived in would pack up our bed clothes into a cart or pram with boxes piled on top and push these contraptions up to the station. Depending where one was going to would determine which station you would have to get out. I hoped it would be London Bridge. No such luck. I had to push ours up to the Elephant and Castle station.

There we would wait to get the hop-picker's special. This was nothing more than the early morning milk train, or post train. One mad rush to get our belongings onto the train and try to find a seat – you'd be lucky. Off we go!

When we got to the farm we children would get out of our parents' way while they went to the farmer's house to get the keys to the huts that they had been allocated. These were no more than a row of sheds. Inside, the walls would be whitewashed and great big bundles of straw were placed so that you could stuff it into your bed linen, complete with clean fresh ticks, these having come off the mattress at home. When this was done and the beds made, mother would begin to hang some curtains around the hut to partition off and make some kind of bedroom apart from the area where we would sit and eat. When the oil lamps were lit it was very cosy and warm inside the hut. Outside we would have a big bonfire going so that the cooking could be done. It was a very happy time sitting round the 'camp-fire' cooking jacket potatoes on the end of a long stick. Bedtime was early as we would have to rise early in the morning to get to the fields and pick a good position for the hop bins.

These were made of wooden trestles which had sacking between the two ends. Into this contraption we would pick the hops from the hop-vine. My father had a pole-pullers job. This meant he would have a section of bins that he looked after. He would be issued with a long pole and if any of the vine was lodged on the upper strings he would have to use this pole to get it down and give it to the person whose row it was in. He also had to see that the floors of the row were picked clean of hops. This is where us kids came in. It was our job, after the bins had moved up the row, to pick all the loose hops from the ground. There would be competition between the children to see how many buckets we could fill. We would get our 'pocket money' for this.

The place that was most popular with our family was a little spot in Kent called Offham. This place was particularly well known as it had on its village green one of the very few Quintains in this country. A Quintain is a target for jousting. The farm was called May's Farm.

The first day of picking was always jumpy as it was determined by how the measures were what the pay per bushel would be. It was hoped each year that the price would be better than the previous year. The number of measures a day was four and the farmer's wife would do the measure. She worked as hard as any man. Bending over the bin, push, push, push, in would go the hops and down would go the amount in the bin. We would stand around and peek into the bin and count how many bushels went into the sacks that the polepullers would hold for the measurer: "My mum's got more than your mum".

*Hopping*

"No she ain't – my mum picked more than your mum yesterday."

This was the talk between us kids. We liked the time that the man with the horse and cart would come along to pick up the 'pockets' of hops and load them onto the cart. We would vie with each other to try and get the driver to let us have a go on the cart. If the farmer wasn't about, we might be lucky and get a ride back to the oast house. There we would help the driver unload the cart.

On the second day of picking we would now know what the pay per bushel would be. It might be 3d a bushel. As one, the pickers would gather together and go to the farmhouse to see Mr May the farmer. This was the pickers' strike, as they were not satisfied with the rate. After a while Mr May would compromise with the pickers and back to work they would go. The 'strike' would not last more than a day. This would give the mums a bit more time to tidy up the hop huts or do a bit of shopping.

No one was paid until the end of the hop picking, but every Saturday afternoon there would be a long line of pickers outside the farmhouse lining up to get a 'sub'. This would be deducted at the end of the season. Sometimes, if you had not picked well, there would be very little to come at the end, after you had subbed most of it to get food or go to the Red Lion at the weekend.

To us kids it was a lovely time. No school – just going for walks and then doing some scrumping. You don't see the 'hopping apples' today. These were nearly as big as your head – or so it seemed to us – I suppose the big apples are kept now for some other use. Shame!

Mother used to wear a big pocket around her waist into which she would put the brass tally that would be given to her for every bushel she had taken from her bin. These would be given up to the farmer and the 'tally' put against her name. A man would come round the fields with a tray round his neck selling sweets or fruit. "Can we have some sweets, mum? Go on, let's have some!" This was the cry from the kids. Sometimes it would be answered with "Get orf, you bugger! What yer think I'm made of? Money don't grow on trees!" This would be followed by yelps as some kid got a swipe round the lughole. More often than not they would pay up to get us out of their way so that they could carry on picking.

Going home was one of the happiest and best parts of 'going hopping'. We would all gather at West Malling station and when we loaded up onto the train we would start singing all the old songs. Us kids would have our own songs like "When You Go Down Hopping Knock at Number One", "See Old Mother Riley", etc.

When we arrived home, a good bath was one of the first things. "School on Monday for you, me lad", my mother would say. "Can't I 'ave another week, mum? Go on, let's have another week", I would cry. Mother was strong willed against my entreaties. But then my whining would be short lived as my mates would knock for me and out I would go to catch up on what had been happening in the neighbourhood during my absence.

## Sunday School: Special Occasions
## Joan Leamy (b. 1913)

At Sunday School every year there were two special events – the "Sunday School Treat" or "Outing" in the summer and the Prize-Giving in the New Year. The most regular place for the "Treat" was Epsom Downs (the "Ups and Downs" as we called it). We travelled by train from Peckham Rye Station, taking our picnic lunch with us – and in a good many cases there was not much lunch left by the time we arrived at the Downs.

The grown-ups decided on a suitable place for a "base"; then we were left to eat our lunch, roam around and play until time for tea, which was provided in a large barn-like structure adjacent to the railway station. After tea there were organised races – egg and sppon, three-legged, sack races etc. Then we all sat on the grass while someone thanked God for our happy day and we sang some of the well-known children's hymns. Afterwards back we came on the train, an old "puffing billy" throwing out smoke and grit, which was likely to get in the eyes of children who would stick their heads out of the windows, despite the efforts of teachers to keep them in!

Other places we visited on our outings were Abbey Woods, Bushey Park etc.

The other annual occasion, the prize-giving, was in three parts. First there was a games period in the lower hall, when we played "Oranges and Lemons", "Sally-go-round-the-moon" etc. Then upstairs for tea, where five or six long tables were laid out. Long sheets of "lining paper" were used as table-cloths to save washing (someone was sure to upset a cup of tea!) Plates of bread and jam were consumed, with tea poured from large blue enamel pots, then madeira and fruit cake and "Playbox" biscuits.

After tea we moved downstairs again; the evening session consisted of singing and recitations by the various classes, a talk by a visiting speaker and distribution of the much-awaited prizes. In those days the prizes were always books, so we just hoped they were duly appreciated by the various boys and girls in the school!

# Chapter Six
# School

## I Could Read at Four
## Alice Cordelia Davis (b. 1898)

I could read when I was four years old, before I went to school. I remember a few houses from where I lived was a house with a large notice in the window. The notice said 'Blind Maker' – I thought that it meant they made blind men.

I started school at four and a half years of age. We were taught reading, writing and arithmetic. The number of children in each class was high, usually about fifty, but I do not remember any trouble, like rudeness, shouting, etc. We progressed to the upper school at about eight years.

I loved reading, but books were not easily obtainable for me, as my mother could not afford to give me the one penny a month which was charged at the Public Library. At the Sunday School I attended there was a library of a kind. There were religious books with gilt edges smelling of mildew, but I read all I could manage. The stories were always sad. Someone always died and was taken to heaven.

## Oliver Goldsmith School, Camberwell
## James Fulljames (b. 1908)

All of us kids went to Oliver Goldsmith School, which was on the corner of Southampton Street and Peckham Road. It was a big red brick building with high narrow windows. There were three floors. Ground floor was infants, middle floor girls and top floor boys.

I, like all the other kids I knew, started school when I was four. My teacher was a Miss Bell, a short, plump, middle aged lady, with a heart of gold and a voice like a fog horn. She was my teacher right through infant school, that is, from four to eight years old. I don't remember very much about those early days. It was all plasticine, cutting up coloured paper to make things, painting, fairy tales, doing simple sums, tables and starting to read. And singing: Jack and Jill, Little Bow Peep, and Three Blind Mice. I was always good at reading. It just came naturally, probably because Mum and Dad were always at it. I remember one incident. I couldn't write down a half and settled for "RF", which Miss Bell seemed to find amusing and showed to everyone.

Another thing I remember was Empire Day, because little though we were, we all marched round the play-ground behind the boy scouts band with arms swinging and heads held high past the big white flag pole to salute 'our flag'. Better still, on Empire Day we all had the afternoon off from school. We all, or nearly all, wore white and were plastered all over with red, white and blue rosettes. Truly a wonderful day. The older girls, or 'The Big Girls' as they were called, were dressed in the national costumes of England, Wales, Scotland and Ireland and gave displays of dancing and singing; the 'Big Boys' did marching and gymnastics. All the local mums crowded into the play-ground to watch.

At one time I sat next to a girl who was constantly wetting her drawers; at times she smelt something 'orrible. When it got too bad I was obliged to raise my hand and tell Miss Bell "She's done it again Miss", whereupon Miss Bell would come galloping over, take a cautious sniff at the offender and detail another little girl to "take her to the lavatory", which I could never understand, 'cos the damage had been done.

At Christmas we had a party in the hall and a big Christmas tree with lots of coloured lights on it. Every kid was presented with a toy, but the only thing I remember getting was a little white tent with a Red Indian standing in the door-way. I suppose it was worth about a tanner, but I thought the world of it and kept it for years.

At the age of eight we really started to live and moved upstairs into the 'Big Boys' school, which was on the top floor. There were six classes, ranging from two to seven. Seven really, 'cos part of Seven was called Ex-Seven.

I can still, after all these years, remember most of the teachers' names. There was Miss Horton, the Art teacher, who was a real 'smasher' and admired by all us boys; Dickie Richards, who taught History and came to school on a bike; Mr Hoile was the Science teacher; Mr Francis Music; Mr Barton taught Geography; and Daddy Ascot, who took the scholarship class, was a real terror. Or so we thought. The Headmaster was a Mr Mollett and before him a Mr Linnaker. Mr Moore taught Carpentry in the big workshop on the far side of the playground and his assistant was a Mr Steele. The caretaker was a Mr Wood.

Dickie Richards was a stern man and all for discipline, but if he did anything to upset us, we waited till school was over, nipped round to the bike shed and let his tyres down.

Mr Hoile taught very elementary Physics and Chemistry. He used to sling bits of chalk at us if we weren't paying attention and he was a real good shot. He wore a wig, as they were called then, and in consequence was nick-named Wiggy Hoile.

Mr Francis took us in singing lessons, which were held in the Hall and we used to enjoy it. We had a school choir and took part in the annual competition that was held in the Masonic Hall in Camberwell New Road, but we never won anything.

Daddy Ascot was a real demon, or so he seemed to us; he taught the scholarship class, which was standard five. I can honestly say that I got the stick off him every day, but I don't think less of him for that; no doubt I deserved it. He was very like the schoolmaster in Goldsmith's "Deserted Village'. "And if severe in aught, the love he bore for learning was at fault". At that time I could, and did, recite the whole of it; even now I remember quite a lot and number it among my favourites. As I said, I was always in his bad books and not without cause.

I recall the occasion when I dipped a piece of chalk in the ink-well and wrote some very rude words in the history book. And it wasn't in tiny letters. It was spread all over the page. Unfortunately the books were collected up before I had time to erase them; the next time they were given out, some toffee-nosed orphan got hold of it and took it to Daddy Ascot. Well, the old boy nearly had a fit and threatened us all with Hell's Fire and Damnation if the boy who did it didn't own up. A kid named Wally Jordan jumped up and said "Fulljames done it, sir. I was sitting behind him and I saw him do it!" Ascot wagged his finger at me and out to the front I go. It was almost dinner time and he said, "Right, my boy. Home to dinner and when you get back, I'll have a policeman waiting for you!" Well, I went home to dinner and on the way back I had visions of going to prison, the chain gang, even of being hung; when I got there, much to my relief there was no sign of a policeman. But it didn't end there. The worst was yet to come.

Old Ascot opened the book at the rude word page and stuck it open with strips of gummed paper. He cast a baleful eye on me and said, 'Now, my boy, you can take this round to every class in the school and show it to every teacher. You can start off with the Head Master."

Even after all that there was more to come. Next morning at prayers in the Hall, I was called out by the Head Master, who, after telling the school what a wicked boy I was, gave me six handers, three on each palm.

But Daddy Ascot did his damndest to cram enough into us to gain a scholarship. He had high hopes of me, but I let him down. I failed in History, but qualified for a place at a Central School, as they were called. Well, I wasn't all that keen and Dad didn't push me, so I stayed on at Oliver Goldsmith. I went up into six and on to Seven and Ex-Seven.

Dickie Barton took Seven and I got on well with him. He taught geography. He must have travelled a lot in his time and would hold forth on all sorts of things that were not in the Geography book. Deserts and jungles, the Amazon and the Nile; we would sit there spell-bound, lapping it all up. He would tell us all about himself and his travels and we recognised in him a kindred spirit, who would far rather rough it than teach in school. I came top of his class for the last three terms, but was never awarded a prize. On each occasion marks for conduct let me down. I tell a lie. A separate prize was awarded for purely Religious Knowledge and I won a beautiful Bible, with limp leather covers, gilt edges and lettering and a section of coloured Biblical maps, a truly handsome book, which I afterwards flogged to brother Jack for half a crown to buy fireworks with.

I mustn't forget Mr Moore, who taught us Woodwork. We attended one day a week and the class was held in the big brick built workshop on the far side of the Boys' playground. Other schools attended there too and we all looked forward to their days, 'cos there was always a real set-to between us during the playtime break. It eventually reached the stage when it was decided to give us separate breaks and the visitors were allotted a break following ours.

Old Moore was a craftsman and everything had to be done just so. First we had to draw the article we were going to make, plan, elevation and side view. Next the wood was planed, marked out, cut to size and shape, glued together, sand papered, stained and polished. At various stages Old Moore would inspect your work; if it didn't measure up to his standards, he'd either rap you over the head with it or sling it from one end of the shop to the other, saying "Rubbish! Break it up for fire-wood!" A real good man for the job. They don't make 'em like that anymore, worse luck.

## Fair Street School, Bermondsey
## Harry Hawes (b. 1922)

Playtime at Fair Street School in Bermondsey in the thirties was Bedlam, as the lads played their favourite game of smashing each other's faces in or playing football with a pupil's new cap. We were a scruffy lot. Oliver Twist and the Artful Dodger looked smarter than us. Around the playground teachers were placed in strategic positions like warders at Dartmoor preventing an escape. In the middle of one punch-up a teacher grabbed me by the ear whilst another pounced on my opponent. During the dinner hour a makeshift ring was arranged so we could slog it out with the gloves on; it wasn't half as much fun, but the ring was to become a regular feature of our school life.

If I had a talent, it was for getting into trouble. One time that stands out in my memory was the school visit to Crystal Palace by train, when it was suggested we should pull the communication cord. Guess who volunteered? The headmaster, known as Banger, devised a fiendish punishment. Next day during morning prayers I was to spend the whole time with my head in the wastepaper basket – with the rest of the rubbish.

One of our regular school journeys was to take outdoor lessons at Bellingham. The trip was by tram and as there were a few boys with new school caps to be broken in it wasn't long before they were flying all over the place. The fun ended when a cap busted one of the light bulbs. I got the blame of course.

Once a week we had Musical Appreciation in the School Hall and, to lads brought up on Henry Hall and Harry Roy who thought that chamber music came from Poland the whole session was a terrific bore. Beethoven was one of the teacher's favourites but to us lads his music was torture, like being punished for a crime you hadn't committed. I was to learn later that Beethoven was deaf and never had to listen to it.

Bookbinding was one of the crafts taught at Fair Street. We had a steel ruler and a sharp knife to cut the cardboard straight and clean, but the only straight and clean cut that I made was on my thumb; I was rushed to Guys Hospital to have it stitched – I still carry the scar as a reminder.

Whilst the master was out of the room I used to entertain the rest of the class by apeing him. Once he came back and caught me redhanded and said he liked a good laugh so I could stand on his desk and entertain him as well.

It was not much fun to have a name like Harry Hawes, especially with a teacher like "the Colonel", who made me march around the classroom saying: "I say Harry the Horse had his Oats" and whacked me with his cane every time I dropped an H or put one in the wrong place. Think it's easy? Then try it!

The school doctor said I needed building up and put me on a diet of school milk, which I never had to pay for. I have never been able to drink milk, so made a deal with a friend. He drank my milk whilst we spent his milk money on sweets. This was to go on for ages, until the doctor decided that the free milk had done its job and took me off it, a sad day.

One of my schoolfriend's parents managed a baker's shop and on leaving the premises Georgie invited me to help myself to a cake. But next day at school I was ordered to the Headmaster's study to explain why I had stolen it. I protested my innocence and in the end my pal owned up to the truth.

Like all schools we had our bully, a little bloke, but very tough. One day it was my turn and he challenged me to a fight in front of my friends. Like the man who proposed to his wife in a garage, I couldn't back out. To my surprise, as the fight progressed, I began to get on top and was belting into him, encouraged by my friends, when some workmen who were passing by pulled me off and let him run away, telling me off for hitting a smaller lad.

# High School? No, said Mum
## Rose Hawkins

I was born in Cornwall Road, SE1, which was part of the Duchy of Cornwall, Crown property. We were very poor. Although my father had a good job, the money went on drink. Mother had the leavings. Things did not get better. My father was an intelligent man – my mother told us that way, way back his family had been wealthy, but it had all gone in drink.

When I started school, we were all intelligent and outstanding both in looks and character; but the dreadful state we had to go to school in – all raggity and dirty! Yet I was the most brilliant girl in the school and by some strange fate, I had to be the strongest swimmer. I remember one teacher saying, "We have not only a genius here; we have a great sportswoman". But she was wrong; I hated netball and other games – could not stand all that pushing and rough stuff.

I spent most of my young girlhood in the public library. I loved books and, by the time I was 12 years old, I had read all the Bronte works, Dickens and a lot of Greek mythology. Anyway, it was warm in the library – we had little or no fire at home. Then I would go to my dear grandmother and she would give me a cup of tea and a slice of bread.

I used to mix with other girls. In the summer we would play at Archbishop's Park and go around to the Lambeth Palace. I remember looking at those doors, centuries old, and touching them. Then we would climb over William Bligh's tomb, the commander of the 'Bounty'. Poor old Bill, they made sure that he was not going to get up again.

Time at school passed and when I was almost 14 years old the time came for me to leave, to put away my history books.

My mother should have come to the school to go before a committee. They wanted me to continue education, but in those days there were no grants, etc. Had it been today, it would have been different. How I would have loved to have gone to a High School! But Mum refused the offer, in spite of the wisdom of other people. "No", she said. I was needed to go to work, as the money was wanted. There was much unemployment in those days. The only job they offered me was at a waste paper sorting factory. It was filthy. I could only stay a few weeks, then came job after job; each one I was not suited to.

Time went on and I met my husband and we were married. I was seventeen years old. My mother in law gave us a room in her house, where my first three children were born. Times were still hard. I would sit up all night and make a blouse for someone, to get a few shillings for food the next day. Yet we were happy together; although he was out of work, he was a good man and a loving husband and father in those days.

## Cator Street School, Peckham
## Leslie Piper (b. 1908)

I had only an elementary education, as it was then called, at Cator Street School, in Peckham. This was a large school for that time, on three floors, with one entrance in Cator Street and one in East Surrey Grove. It had two playgrounds, one for the boys and the other for the girls and infants.

The old school has gone, being destroyed in the Second World War by bombs.

All things considered, I had a happy school life; I was by no means a brilliant academic student, but always finished somewhere in the top half. I loved sports and played for the school at cricket and football, besides being a close third in the school at running.

Our old headmaster was something of a tyrant and there was no organised sport during his 'reign'. When he retired, much to our joy, we had a much more sympathetic man in his place. He got us interested in sport and used to give talks to us older boys, which were very helpful. He was a strict man, but he was also very fair; we boys all liked him and no-one thought of taking advantage of him. Perhaps we appreciated him more, for being such a contrast to his predecessor.

One activity in the snowy weather was the snowball "war" against other schools. Large numbers of us would roam the streets after school hoping to meet a rival gang. As soon as identity was established, a snowball battle would begin and the air would be thick with missiles. Anyone unlucky enough to be captured would have to endure the "torture" of snow being put down their necks. All quite innocent fun, if a trifle uncomfortable, but there was certainly no violence or "aggro" in those days.

## St George's National School, Camberwell
## Lilian Blore (b. 1905)

Four generations of my family went to St George's National School, starting with my father. I started in the infant school. Miss Bull was headmistress when I was five years old. My sister Caroline had gone into the big girls' school. She was nine years old. When I was seven I went up, too. Mrs Gooding was headmistress there. Mr Gooding, her husband, was headmaster in the boys' school.

Our domestic teacher, Miss Shilling – I didn't like her at all. She would come and stand over us whilst we were knitting and always found fault; I would go all tense and couldn't do anything right. She never gave us any encouragement. After I left school I was a very good knitter and partly earned my living by it.

When I was in the fourth class, Miss Phillips was my favourite teacher. My best subjects were drawing, composition, reading, knitting and scripture. Miss Phillips helped me a lot and advised me about my drawings. She was very interested in them. I always got top marks every week, ten out of ten. She would say to me "If only someone could teach you more about drawing. You almost bring your paintings to life". In those days when I went to school there were no arts and crafts classes, so my gift for painting was wasted.

We never had outings like the schools hAve today. The girls never went swimming, only the boys.

I always looked forward to Empire Day. All the girls wore white, with white shoes and stockings, a piece of red, white and blue ribbon to tie in our hair and a small Union Jack. Afterwards it was put away until the next year.

In the school, on religious days, all the children would go to St George's Church for a service. Then we would go back to school for a few lessons and have half a day's holiday. We always had six weeks holiday every year. St George's School was destroyed by bombing in the World's Second War.

# Scarsdale Road School, Camberwell
## Stan Hall (b. 1910)

My first contact with books and learning was our family Bible. Perhaps not so many people read Bibles today. Every house would have one when I was a child. I think one thought that the larger the Bible displayed in the 'front room', the better Christian you were, not withstanding the fact that fifty per cent of the population could not read. My own Mother could neither read nor write. She was unable to sign her name. She made her 'mark', which was an 'X'. Although she could not read, she was a very able person. Her appearance was good; she was a Victorian who had seen how the better off people behaved in the clubs she had worked in. She was always fresh and clean looking, held herself upright to her five feet nine and had very good manners. It was years before I realised she could not read. Although my Father always read the newspapers to her, I thought he was just doing what each head of the house did. Many people who could write entered all the main dates of the family on the first page of the family Bible: birthdays, marriages, deaths etc. My Father had left school at the ripe old age of twelve years and had taught himself further, enough to get by. But it wasn't until his later life that he had the time to enjoy a good book. He did a lot to encourage me to read also, although I wasn't aware, as I watched him read, that I was watching a starving man with the 'hunger of learning' in his reading.

My Mother had led an appalling childhood. Hardships and hunger being no stranger to her, she had made up her mind that the schooling she had lost I would not; and certainly ill health was not going to be the cause of my missing school. In 1915 I was five and old enough to start. I understand that I cried all day the first day and even the rocking horse would not shut me up, although I spent all day on it. I was at last sent home in the company of an older girl. They perhaps hoped I would not return the next day, but my Mother had ways of making you do things. Next day she took me right into the classroom and warned me of what might happen if the performance was repeated.

My school was the Scarsdale Road School of the School Board of London, a large, box-like building with infants on the ground floor, older girls on the first floor and older boys on the top.

My Mother's regard for my health decided that I should have school milk. Yes, it was possible, even in 1914; if the family could afford it, for one farthing (a tenth of the new penny) a third of a pint of milk would be delivered to the school and find its way to my classroom. The milk was contained in a pewter container with a brass top flag, and a thin brass handle by which to hold it. In the classroom, as well as the fireplace at the front of the room was a large tortoise stove which burned coke. My milk – I was the only child whose parents had made the effort or could afford to pay the farthing – was placed on the stove to warm. By the time break came there was a thick layer of yellow fat on the top of the milk (milk was not treated then). My teacher supervised the drinking of it, telling me how lucky I was. I hated the stuff; I wished that the other poor hungry kids, who eyed it longily, could have had it. My second year, with a change of teacher, I stopped having this 'special treat'. I've hated milk ever since.

Classes were graded in Standards, which meant I suppose the standard of your education. At the end of each year an examination was held to observe if you were bright enough to be transferred to the next Standard; if not you stayed behind in that Standard and mingled with the group that were moving up. There were cases of children leaving in the 5th standard, but the usual length of schooling was seven years in the big boys, standards 1 to 7. They could not hold too many back, as the classes were already in the sixty per class numbers.

My first two years was in standard 1 and 2, the teacher a Mr Woffington, 'Woffy' among the boys. He was, or was supposed to be, almost stone deaf. He must have been excellent at lip reading because he could catch you out talking. Sometimes he would call you out and accuse you of talking, when in fact he had caught you chewing, but it was all the same to him – he'd caught you. He was a great one to set you work to do in the morning. He would then pull open the drawer of his desk, in which he had carefully spread his newspaper. He could even turn the pages without taking out the paper. Sometimes, should he not have seen out of the corner of his eye the headmaster approaching, he nearly shut his fingers in closing the drawer smartly.

All teachers had canes, which they used several times per day, some much more than others. Not only did you get caned for discipline reasons, but also for bad work. How this helped to improve your work was not clear. The headteacher on his rounds always carried his cane and could find reasons to use it. I arrived at school late one moring, though I had an excellent record for punctuality. You were not allowed into the classroom whilst the register was being called. The headmaster appeared and asked what I was doing outside the door. I confessed I was late. I was ordered to hold out each hand in turn and received a stroke of the cane on each – not exactly a stroke, more a pile driver. The reason for my lateness was that my Mother had had a haemorrhage that morning and was vomiting blood. I had been in the house on my own with her, but, being the tough person she was, she had got me to call the woman in the house opposite and soon I was bundled off to school very frightened.

The highlight of the year was Empire Day. In my second year (I was six years old then) we were dressed up as the countries of the Empire, mostly by the use of coloured crêpe paper. The colour would be of the particular country's flag. Those of us that should have had brown or black faces received them. I have a very faded photograph of the event. I was representing Montenegro. Not only did I not know who or where that was, but I couldn't even say the word. Anyway, the teachers had fun.

In the Big Boys we had to clean up for the day. Boys actually did wash that day.

117

Although on ordinary days we had inspections for the washing of face and hands, and providing it was possible, hair combing, this only meant half the class in the washroom looking at the water and returning to the promise of the cane 'next time'. For Empire Day the clothes had to have a good brushing and a clean shirt had to be worn. It was no good the teachers requesting "Your best suit" or "School Uniform"; nobody had school uniform and seventy-five per cent had only what clothes they came to school in. Some made the effort by wearing their father's best shirt; some even had the front cut out of an old shirt to wear as a 'Dickie', but collars and ties? Don't be silly! I have a picture taken of our class on Empire Day, all sixty-three of us. Four boys are wearing shirts and I was the only one with a white one. The other fifty-nine were wearing torn and mended jumpers, some even a cut down Army jacket which had been their father's or brother's.

For the Big Boys Empire Day, a platform was erected in the playground and during the afternoon we all assembled in front of it. Our Mothers, or rather those that were not out earning a penny or two, not busy doing the washing that they 'took in', not drunk, or not disinterested, gathered to one side. Some man came to present the prizes, three books supplied by the School Board for London. I never knew what they were or for what they were given, I never got one – The man, whoever he was (I think he was a Councillor who rarely ventured out in public other than on election day once a year) would make a long speech which meant little to us even if we could hear him, then would present the prizes and the headteacher would give his once a year smile. We would all sing 'Land of Hope and Glory', not that many had much hope and would receive precious little glory; then a couple of verses of 'O Lord of Life', especially the bit about 'In danger on the sea', then 'God Save the King' and that was that for another year.

The last five years of my schooling were spent in another classroom. The teacher was a Mr Morris, another teacher who never smiled, although I did find out in the last year he had left us because of stomach troubles. He had us for three years and was replaced by another for the last two years, a Captain Saxon, who had left the army and taken up teaching. We also had a new headmaster, who did bring a breath of fresh air with him. Our teacher was a B.Sc, so the new head arranged a change in the school programme. He would take two other Standards for one afternoon for science and his own of course. We would have a special class on one of these days for History and another for Geography. Another day we went to a school nearby for Woodwork, so the first specialist teaching was beginning. But what a task that was! They still had half-starved badly clothed children, who along with their parents, were not very interested in their future.

There were Health Inspection days, more like a visit to the ear, nose and throat hospital; teeth were dealt with by another inspection; and then there was 'Nitty Nora', a nurse who would have the children lined up and go through each child's hair with a steel comb which was dipped frequently into a small white enamel bowl, kidney shaped. Towards the end of the period the contents, which had been clean water carbolic, looked more like the 'Soup of the Day'. Each child having their head examined almost shook with fear. If there were nits there, they were taken off and with others so affected their hair was all cut off, the head shaved and treated with ointment. The girls would wear a kind of pudding clothing over their bald head; the boys, one of their father's caps, or even their own, which would, without any hair, drop over their eyes. It wasn't so much that you had nits it was the humiliation of the head shaving and everyone knowing why. It was like people having bugs or mice. Everyone had them, but nobody would admit to it. Fortunately I did not suffer the nit ordeal, but my wife tells me she did; it is a lasting memory for her.

Each classroom was alike, with a table with one drawer for the teacher, a cupboard, a blackboard and a fireplace to the front of the room, which the teacher sat near. If you were a big child, as I was, you sat at the back and it was very cold. There was often a large picture of Edward the Seventh above the fireplace. There were not enough of these to go around, so some had Queen Victoria, some even had the old classic 'The Stag at Bay'; even this was a picture with a scene, better than the other two staring down at you.

As I said, because we had not got facilities for a woodwork room at the Scarsdale Road School, we had to attend another school in Coburg Road. This was a subject that I really enjoyed. The teacher at this school was so impressed by how I had progressed in a short time that he considered I might make a Woodwork teacher. He contacted my headmaster and an interview was arranged

*An exam*

for me to attend the Shoreditch Technical Training College for Teachers. I did pass the entrance exam and was accepted, but, on discussion with my parents, the fact that I would have to attend the college for another seven years meant my parents keeping me, clothing me and covering all expenses; as they were now both in their fifties, that dream faded.

There was still the last year's exams for further education. One child could go to Wilson's Grammar School, two to the Secondary School in Mina Road and there was one place at the Technical Trade School. There was just one snag; there were sixty-three boys in our Standard Seven and only four places, even if parents could afford to keep their son at school when there were millions unemployed. There were no percentage passes then; only the top of the exam got the place.

So in 1924 I left the school where I learned first to make numbers and letters on a slate with a slate pencil and was taught to sharpen the slate pencil on the stone sharpener fitted to the school wall, progressing to the use of pen and ink. Most of the ink went on our fingers. We were also taught mental arithmetic, a lost art today. With fifty-nine other boys I left for the great outside world, where few of us would get jobs. Fortunately, I was one of the lucky ones.

# The Cold Hinge Treatment
## Alf Slater (b. 1927)

I rubbed my hand on the cold comforting iron hinge on the top of my desk. The veterans of many past "Handers" had always told me that it took the sting away and helped to suppress the sausage-like weal that emerged across the palm of your hand. I'm glad that I never drew my arm in slightly as that whispy piece of venom flashed through the air, because if it had landed on my fingers, I'd have had four "little dollies" to bother about. I wasn't very impressed with the Cold Hinge Treatment. My hand still hurt; in plain language "It hurt a bloody lot!" "Sod this!" I thought. "I won't be late again. I'll be an early morning coward in future". I had just experienced that very important aspect of school discipline in those days, the cane. I cannot and will not comment on its value; all I can say is it certainly deterred me.

It is without malice or bitterness that I commence my episode of school life with something as traumatic as being caned. It is just coincidental. My real awareness of school began with my elevation to the junior section. The only memory I have of the genteel infant portion of my schooling is a great reluctance to attend and the morning ritual of a bucket of tears. And then, of course, there was the day I messed my trousers and had to be taken home. The infant portion of my schooling was not very appealing to me or the teachers.

The school I attended for the whole of my school life was St Joseph's, in Pitman Street, Camberwell. It was a large square building of three floors, with a playground on the roof. One started in the Infants on the ground floor at five years of age and at fourteen you left to start work. The school life was nine years, almost equally divided into these three floors. There was a scholarship examina- tion at eleven. If you passed you were given a chance to attend a secondary school of higher education and to remain there until you were sixteen, but for many of the children that did pass, it was a wasted effort, because the majority of parents could not afford the cost of the uniform or the lack of income from their children for a further two years.

St Joseph's is a Catholic school; the religious connection therefore was very strong – and you had a few more religious holidays as well. These were called 'Holidays of Obligation'. You were expected to go to church – and you did.

The level of teaching was basic, good and adequate – although not very varied. Such things as projects, Social Studies and the wider aspects of Science and Biology teaching were very much in the future. The general elements of learning were confined to the basic three 'R's: Reading, Writing and Arithmetic. There were also History and Geography lessons, but as far as I was concerned they only confirmed that the "Battle of Hastings" was in 1066 and that the earth was round . . . But perhaps that was my fault.

*Alf Slater's childhood friends*

"You'll never be as clever as your brother", said the teacher as he brought the geography book thudding down on my head. This highlighted another aspect of school at that time, the eternal comparison with other members of your family; it could be your brother, sister, uncle, even your father. Whole families followed each other. Teachers also stayed at the same school for many years. This was particularly true of St Joseph's. Both sides were therefore able to get to know each other's reflex actions very well. Although my head had a few more encounters with the book of knowledge, I never allowed myself to test the theory of the cold hinge treatment again – it didn't work anyway.

# Chapter Seven
# Going to Work

## Ermine and Persian Lamb
## Alice Cordelia Davis (b. 1898)

It was January 1912. I was fourteen years old; my birthday was on the Friday and I started work on the Monday. To me it was thrilling. I had put my hair 'up' – it was very long and thick. My mother took me to see about a job. I was to "learn a trade" and was engaged to a dyers and cleaners shop. My uniform was a black sateen apron.

Learning the trade consisted of taking the owner's two small children to school and taking special orders. The shop where I worked was in the midst of theatrical boarding houses. It was, you will remember, the time of the music halls. Sometimes our customers would need a very quick cleaning job, such as dress suits, dresses and sometimes furs. Ermine tippets were very popular and I was always fascinated when a real ermine tippet (which was a narrow little fur with black tails) came in to be cleaned. One day we had to clean a real Persian lamb coat; this had to be insured.

In the shop was a telephone box. After the girl had obtained your number you put tuppence in the slot. I can still remember the number: Hop. 3094, but I do not think there is such an exchange now.

My wage for 'learning the trade' was two shillings and sixpence a week. I worked from 8.30am to 7.30pm. Most of the time I was quite happy, except for sometimes on a Monday when I had to act as a van-boy. On this day the owner of the shop went to the West End to collect work. He had a small horse-driven cart and I was left to sit in front whilst he went into the flats and houses. The horse was rather thin and seemed to know I was nervous of him because he would turn around and look at me, giving a deep shudder and a neigh.

Lots of good things came out of working at the shop, because I enjoyed the shop's own reading matter: the Gem, the Magnet, the Trade Journal and the Union Jack. These magazines I avidly read whilst eating my dinner in the shop parlour. Sometimes I had to go to the nearby public house to get a bottle of whisky – I remember there was the design of a shamrock on the label.

Occasionally I was very lucky and would get a tip of two or threepence from a customer.

# Office Work to Factory Floor
## Lil Blore (b. 1905)

I was fourteen years old in June 1919. My sister Caroline was working for a firm called Croppers Ltd in Southwark Bridge Road. She worked in the Manager's Office. My sister asked the Manager if he could find a job for me. I was to start when I left school. A new law had been passed saying no-one could leave school until the end of each term. So instead of leaving in June I left in August, when the six weeks holidays started. My mother was disappointed. She was waiting for the money that I was to earn. Before the law was passed you could leave the same week as your birthday.

I started work on the Monday after leaving school on the Friday. I was put in the Manager's office and my sister was in the big general office. I started at 16 shillings a week. My mother gave me 3 shillings a week pocket money. She bought my clothes out of the money I gave her. I bought my stockings out of my pocket money. The cheap stockings were 6¾d a pair and the dearer stockings were 11¾d a pair; if the shopkeepers did not have farthings for change they could give you a packet of pins to make up for the money.

The Manager's name was Mr Mayhew where I worked. Every Monday to Friday and half day Saturday I went by tram. If you went before eight o'clock you would get a return ticket for 2d to Southwark Bridge. The hours were from half past eight until half past five in the evening, Saturday half past eight to one o'clock. The workers in the factory all started at eight o'clock in the morning. We never had summer holidays, only Bank Holidays. And it was only after years that we got paid for Bank Holidays. It was stopped out of our wages before. I worked for Croppers Ltd for three years. They made cardboard boxes.

In 1922 Croppers decided to move to Newbury owing to the high rates in London. My sister Caroline had met her husband at the firm. He was a fitter and looked after the machinery. They had not been married very long when Croppers moved, putting my sister me and my brother-in-law out of work. My sister after a time went for a job at R. White's Ltd, a confectionery firm in New Church Road, Camberwell. Owing to my sister getting a job, my brother-in-law took one pound four shillings a week dole and I took fifteen shillings. One Friday when we went to get our money it had been lowered. My brother-in-law took fifteen shillings and I took ten shillings.

I was out of work for six months and my brother-in-law for two years. We both tried to look for work but there were no jobs about. As my sister was at work she was not allowed any dole money with her husband's dole money. In the end Caroline heard at R. White's that they wanted more workers. I was getting on for eighteen years old.

I worked for them for ten years and in all that time we never got more money given us. I had the same wages when I left as when I began working for them. It was very hard work for both me and my sister after being in an office, but it was all we could get. We both started with 27 shillings a week with one shilling stopped for a stamp, making 26 shillings clear. One day all the employees decided to come out on strike. The boss was told we were coming out for more money. We all went to a meeting in one of the workrooms. He told us if we went out on strike, we would be dismissed, as plenty of other people were waiting for work. Despite this, looking back, it was the happiest time in my life. This was why we continued to work for the same money all those years. The women were the salt of the earth. We were all poor. We would all help one another. If we borrowed money we always paid back what we had borrowed when we got our wages. We were always singing or laughing, for no-one was better off than the other.

The hours began to get longer and with the overtime at the end of the week we took one pound ten shillings. The hours were from eight o'clock in the morning till one, one hour's break, then from two o'clock to eight o'clock at night, Monday to Friday. On Saturdays it was eight o'clock until one o'clock break then on until five o'clock, with ten minutes break for lunch and ten minutes for tea. It was the law to have breaks for a meal. We had nowhere to hang our outdoor clothes – we just put them in the room where we worked. Mr Herbert White, one of the shareholders, was very concerned about the hours we worked, especially the married women; he did not know how they managed with their chores at home, but they did. They nearly all worked near the firm and in the lunchtime errand girls were allowed to go out and buy some food. We would have rolls at four a penny, with a ¼lb corned beef and a ¼ ham. They would make the lunch do and go home and clean as much of their houses as they could, with one eye on the clock to be back by two o'clock. And they would be up early in the morning to do their washing before going to work.

Woolworth's were giving R. White's big contracts for their confectionery, so they could have paid us more. Mr Herbert White told our manager and supervisor that he did not have many shares in the firm, so I suppose he could not do anything to help us. I left in the end to have a baby.

## How I went into the Family Trade: Farrier
## Leslie Piper (b. 1908)

I left school in the summer holidays of 1922, as I would have been fourteen before the school resumed. There was a great slump at the time and jobs were very hard to come by, so I was considered lucky to obtain a job straight from school. This job was at a furniture shop midway between New Cross Gate and Old Kent Road station, owned by a Mr Graves. He was a real taskmaster of the old school, a Shylock not satisfied with his pound of flesh, but extracting the last drop of blood as well. My hours were to have been from nine o'clock till eight on four days a week, with a half day on Thursday, and from nine till nine on Saturdays. The starting times were strictly enforced to the very minute, but the finishing times were left to the pleasure and convenience of my employer. My half hour tea break was stopped after a few weeks by the simple expedient of sending me to lunch very late. This one hour break was the only relief I had all day. It took me twenty minutes to get home and the same time to get back; I had to jump a tram and then run all the way home from the stop in Old Kent Road.

I had to walk to and from work each day, but even after a day's hard work this was no hardship, as it was like being released from prison to hear those sweet words "All right, you can go now." It was always around nine o'clock before I got home and on Saturdays after ten, as I was not allowed to leave until the furniture was taken in and that could not be done while there was a customer in the shop. My first duties each morning consisted of cleaning the entrance and the plate glass window and then putting a show of furniture on the shop front, securing the more vulnerable pieces against the wind. Cleaning the window was my greatest trial, as I only had rags and cold water to work with. When I had finished I had to inform the boss, who would then stand close to the window and look all around for smears -- which he invariably found. Then I had to take my rag and remove them until he was finally satisfied. If there was no furniture to be delivered, I had to dust all the furniture on show in the window over and over again. The delivery was done by hand barrow. I had to walk to such places as Bethnal Green and Bow to fetch suites of furniture from the cabinet makers. This meant crossing Tower Bridge or London Bridge and going through the City. There are some very steep hills around New Cross and, although I was very strong, I often had to back the barrow into the kerb in order to have a rest. I was always sent out on Thursday mornings to deliver furniture, usually at long distances, so that I could not get back until after one o'clock. All this for the princely sum of fifteen shillings per week.

It was never intended that I should follow the family profession of horse shoeing, but soon, after a short spell working in a chocolate factory, we had a spell of bad weather. In those days, before horse owners could be persuaded to have screw holes put in their horse shoes to take frost screws, it was the practice to frost nail the shoes as a temporary measure. This entailed removing some nails from the shoes and replacing them with chisel headed nails to enable the horse to get a grip on the snow covered roads. In the case of milk horses and others who had to work over the weekends, the shoes were roughed, usually on Fridays when they had finished their day's work. Roughing lasted for a few days and consisted of removing each shoe, turning down each heel and then nailing the shoe on again. This meant that the horses had to be taken to the forge and it was my first job to fetch and return each pair of horses. I only did this as I was out of work and to help my father to get the work done by not taking away a tradesman for the job. I then did odd jobs at the forge and as nothing turned up for me, I gradually drifted into the job, becoming what will no doubt be the last of a long line of farriers spanning four generations.

If there had been a fall of snow overnight, we would be awakened about three o'clock in the morning. It would be the horsekeeper from the Co-op. We would have to get up and dress, walk to the forge to collect our tools etc. and then walk to the stable, about a mile altogether, and frost nail the horses in the stable. We were saved this job when the shoes were put on with screw holes, as the stablemen or drivers were provided with clearing taps and screws and did the job themselves. We were paid at the rate of threepence per hole, usually three eighths of an inch for a medium-sized horse. The screws were intended to be removed each night to guard against injury and also to prevent the screws from wearing down flush with the shoe, thus preventing extraction with a spanner.

One particularly bad morning, later known as the silver thaw, the snow began to melt and then suddenly froze again. The roads and paths were just like glass and the hospitals were very busy with casualties with broken limbs. Afterwards the streets were littered with old socks and rags that people had tied to their shoes in order to get a grip. My father was the first out that morning. He came back to warn me, as he had slithered down the path to the gate. We put horse nails in the heels of our boots and turned them over to get a grip. We had to walk very gingerly, but were at least able to stay upright.

Although when I went into the farriers' business, horses were on their way out, there were still many smithies in and around Peckham.

My Uncle Harry was dead and my father and Harry's son Will, with a foreman named Bill Miles, were all qualified farriers; I was just a beginner, but by the time we closed the shop in 1941, I was the only farrier left in Peckham and for several miles round. With my father's teaching and a spell at the Borough Polytechnic in shoe making and anatomy, he and I ran the business, now sadly depleted owing to the modernisation of road transport. We had quite a wide variety of horses, including costermongers' ponies, milk horses, undertakers' carriage horses, coal horses and the occasional donkey.

It might be interesting to anyone who cares to read this in the future to mention a few of the prices we charged in those days for a set of shoes: Donkeys 4/-, Ponies 6/-, Cobs 8/- or 9/-, Van Horses 10/-, Cart Horses 12/-. For drawing out, sharpening and tempering cold chisels, all we got was 3d each, and 3d each end for drawing out pickaxes. It was not a very remunerative trade and it did not offer a great return for the very hard work it demanded.

We had quite a few bad debts too and helped to keep down our overheads by making most of our own tools from old rasps, files and spring steel. Our toeing knives for cutting down the horses' feet were made from old bayonets and swords bought for a few pence. We bought some machine made shoes, but when we had time we made as many as possible by hand. These were better as they were usually made for each individual horse, especially for those with bad feet. Some we made by doubling over a big old shoe, welding in a piece to make a good toe and then drawing out the quarters. This was known as "Old Stuff" in the trade and was very, very hard work. The fireman made the shoes, and when there were three of us, my father and I used the sledgehammer; the fireman held the iron and turned it to receive the blow where it was required. Later, when my father and I were on our own, I was the fireman and my father used the sledge and put on the shoe after I had fitted them. The man who nailed on the shoes was known as a doorman; his job was to remove the old shoes and prepare the foot ready for the fireman to fit the shoe.

When one man did everything, as I did after my father died, the job was known as a foot and fire. My father died in 1937 and I carried on, sometimes with part-time help, until 1941 when, after having the shop blasted by bombs on several occasions, and through other difficulties brought about by the war, closed the shop and obtained employment as a farrier with the Express Dairy Co. at Mill Hill.

My father was always a very strong man and seemed almost impervious to pain. One day he received a nasty kick in the mouth while shoeing a horse – incidentally with the new shoe on. Refusing all our offers of help, he held a handkerchief to his mouth and walked the half mile to St. Giles' Hospital for attention. This involved the removal of several teeth through the split in his lip, and then the stitching up of the cut, after which he walked home. This, however, seemed to mark the beginning of the end for him, although he lived for several years and worked until he almost literally dropped. He died a week or so after, in 1937 in his flat in Linden Grove at the age of 68.

When I started work for the Express Dairy Co. at Mill Hill, where they had a smith's shop with four forges on a farm. The fires were blown by electric fans which was strange to me as I had been used to a hand pumped bellows. There were seven or eight farriers there and we mostly used machine made shoes preparing them for the horses we had to shoe later. After our lunch we each packed up our bag of shoes and tools and were taken in a van to our various depots, where we had to do the necessary shoeing, making sure that the horses would be all right until we came the following week. We each had a hundred or so horses to look after and we had to fit the shoes cold. Each depot had a small anvil and we took a heavy hammer with us in order to effect any necessary alterations. The cold shoeing was a war time concession owing to the blackout but it seemed to work quite well and we had little trouble.

## My Route to the Old Kent Road Bus Garage
## Stan Hall (b. 1910)

There were sixty-three of us in my class. When we left school, we had no way to assess the extent of our knowledge of the school subjects, except by the personal remarks made on a School Leaving Certificate which was more designed to notify your future employer that you were "A reliable boy, honest, will make good . . . ". Employers hardly looked at these as I suspect they were more or less all the same.

128

*Unemployed men, 1930's*

I remember well the message given us from the Headmaster as he surveyed us motley group of leavers, realising the small hopes that were before us. "What can I say to you lads", he said, "except to draw to your attention that life is always a gamble and that if I could collect all the wealth in the world and divide it equally amongst you, in a short time some of you would have nothing, whilst others would have doubled their share. So there will always be the have-nots . . .".

Off we went to search a job market that wasn't there. I went to builders and carpentry shops, to many other small works, even to the Docks beside the Thames; that was daily work with the work force selected by the ganger early in the morning and you had to be experienced. But how did you get experienced? I even made an early visit to Smithfield to join the queue of others and to Billingsgate, where the customary shake of head told me there was nothing. But I was in time to see Lower Thames Street being washed down. This was done by a man with a special belt around his middle which had several jets in. A long hose was attached to the belt and the man walked along the street with jets of carbolic water spurting out across the roadway. It certainly cleared away the smell of fish.

I found lots of time to practise the piano and the drums. There was little else to do. There was a boxing club in Albany Road in the Sheldrake Pickle factory, but although I belonged to it and had some fun there, I didn't fancy a bashing once a week. Then I was offered an evening's engagement at a concert. This was only once in two weeks, but the 15/-, even if it did work out to 7/6d a week, possibly might lead to something else.

129

At that time I looked older than my years and could pass as seventeen or eighteen years of age. A man with a saxophone teamed up with my playing at a party and, as we appeared to co-ordinate, he suggested that I should go to a pub where he had arranged an evening of music at the week-end. This was the beginning of music in pubs; some pubs did not have a music licence then. I went, although my parents were not too happy about it, and then got 3/6d each night; but before I could fulfil my next engagement the publican had found out that I was under sixteen, so that finished that.

Then the job. My father came home one day to tell me to report to Old Kent Road Bus Garage in a turning off the Old Kent Road called Bows Road (the GPO now use the old garage as a parcels depot). Off I went the next morning to see the Depot Superintendant, with whom my father had fixed the job. My father, as an inspector, was attached to this Depot. I presented myself to a Mr Dillon, the Superintendant, who duly passed me over to the office manager in the large office attached to the Superintendant's.

The staff consisted of a chief clerk and three clerks; the chief clerk was in his early fifties and had missed the War. The clerks had not: one had been a pilot and had crashed. Although his facial scars were slight, he had, I believe, spent some time in hospital. The second clerk only had one arm; the other he had left in France. The third was poor old Evans, such a nice chap, a fine figure of a man, but he had no toes; these had been frozen in the War and had to be removed. He walked on the balls of his feet. He must have spent a long time learning to do this, as the end of the War was now nearly three years ago.

But it was the chief clerk that was the character. Once a month I was given an address and was told to take an envelope to it, to a woman with the same name as himself. I later found out it was his wife. He lived with a "dolly bird", I was learning. He spent most of the day studying the runners and riders and later giving me a folded piece of paper and a couple of shillings to take to the man at the top of Bowls Road. This was the 'Bookie's Runner', as betting unless licensed was illegal. The runner collected bets under the nose of the law, who would 'run him in' if they caught him. The police had bad eyes for a length of time until occasionally they would take him in with an apology: "Sorry mate, I've got to do you sometimes". The bookmaker would of course pay the runner's fine. I have never backed horses throughout my life and I executed this mission with distaste. The runner would often frighten the life out of me when he suddenly emerged from his 'hidey hole' and said "Do you want me?" flashing side glances in all directions.

It was a long time before I realised where the money for the chief clerk's betting often came from. It was customary for an Inspector to call at the office to inspect the books and the work of the office. Strangely enough the chief clerk had always left the keys of the petty cash box at home. The Inspector would either let it go uninspected or would call again the next day. So the chief clerk would have time to beg, borrow, or steal the money to put the amount right. He kind of lent the cash box money for a short while, to empty it once the Inspector had left.

I was to take over the office boy's job from another lad, who was moving to another job in the Garage. The London General Omnibus Company had a system where they took on a young boy and put him through various sections of the overall system; the boy served an apprenticeship, first by doing the smaller jobs and going on from there.

The boy I took over from was a Len Williams, who was to become my special friend for a number of years. There were of course other youths aged from fifteen to twenty years, who had gone through the system. I discovered, under a week's introduction from Len, that the first job was to collect the mail from this garage and take it to the head office at 55 Broadway, Westminser, there to receive the mail for your garage to bring back. Returning to the office, you had several office tasks to perform and to be a general dogsbody. After a week Len left the Office to take up his new job in the office in the workshop of the garage. My working hours were from 7.30 in the morning until 5.00 in the evening and from 7.30 until 12 noon Saturdays. Everyone worked Saturdays then, except that the office staff and the Garage started at 8.00 in the morning and worked until 5.30 or 12.30 on Saturday.

For my 47 hours I received 3d an hour, which meant that I drew the weekly wage of 11/9d, less 3d for my insurance stamp for my 47 hour week making 11/6d. My mother had 10/- and I received the odd 1/6d.

# In the Print
## Phyllis Hall (b. 1910)

It was 1924, the year of the British Empire Exhibition at Wembley, that I left school, the school leaving age being 14 years of age. Having been with the same teacher for the last six years, I was reluctant to leave; you could, if you wished, stay on for another year, which I had hoped to do, but my parents had said 'NO'. I had to begin to contribute to the family income.

One of my aunts had asked my mother if I could be a nursemaid to her two young children whilst she could continue to work. This was agreed, not from my point of view I might add. My aunt had agreed to pay me a wage, but at the end of the first week my aunt gave me 2/6d. My mother went berserk when I handed her the half crown, had a flaming row with my aunt and that was that. Not that I was sorry; I had to walk four miles to my aunt's home and four miles back each day.

After a few weeks my father met a friend who had a printing works at Blackfriars. He offered me an apprenticeship to the craft of bookfolding which was to take four years. Apprenticeships were the way at that time of obtaining the cheapest form of labour.

When you started at a job like this, the last thing you did was bookfolding. You were just a general dogsbody for starters, making the tea and running the errand for the rest of the factory's needs. Staff canteens hadn't been invented; all we had was an old iron gas stove on the factory floor (it was never cleaned in all the thirteen years I was there).

The forelady was nicknamed 'The Dragon', but called 'Tot' by everyone because of her small size. If she should have a chop or whatever for her lunch, I had to put it in the oven at a set time, scrub a 'spud' and put that in too; if it was not done to a turn at the precise time, I was ridiculed in front of all the staff present. Another job was to clean out vile smelling tins that held about three gallons of glue, used for many reasons in the production of the work. When the tins were empty I had to scrape them out. The remains were caked hard and smelled really foul, but woe betide you if you didn't get the tin clean, as it had to be returned clean to the suppliers. The forelady would call me "the manageress of the paste tin". We had some old cups for putting in the glue from the tins for use in the factory. The first time I made the tea for the staff (another of my general duties), I poured it into these glue cups, thinking they were the cups used for tea. This was another opportunity for 'The Dragon' to ridicule me with all the staff looking on.

The forelady's name was Miss Vale. She sat on a raised platform so that she could have her beady eye on everyone. Talk if you dare – she would be on you like a ton of bricks. She would cross over to where you were working and tell you to stop talking and get on with your work. She did this with the action of prodding you in the back with a bony finger on each word.

I hated the Wilkes Brothers and Greenwood factory. When I first started the staff were typical factory types. They told blue jokes and used bad language, which I have never been able to accept. Because I refused to join in, they christened me the "Parson's Daughter".

My mother would take eight of the nine shillings and ninepence I received each week. I would have the odd one shilling and ninepence. It was a 48 hour week, at 2½d per hour; 3d was stopped for National Insurance which made my take home pay nine shillings and nine pence.

For my one shilling and ninepence, I had to pay 6d compulsory union dues and 6d for a cup of tea at work (eleven cups for 6d). This left me with ninepence for myself for my 48 hours of purgatory. I received for myself 0.15 of a new penny per hour.

When we got very busy we had to do eight hours per week overtime, which made a 56 hour week, giving me an extra one shilling and tenpence per week. I was rich! My mother would give me 6d for my fare and lunch. It was 2d return on the 'Workman's' tram from Peckham to Blackfriars; my lunch was 2oz of corned beef for 2½d and one pennyworth of chips. With the odd halfpenny I would buy a cake or an apple. This would have to be eaten at the work bench. Some of the work would entail standing the eight or nine hours at a monotonous and repetitive job, plus the racket of the noisy machinery.

We were always short of cash in our house and it was a search for money to get to work by the end of the week. One Friday my mother gave me her last sixpence for my fare and lunch. When I got on the tram after a mad scramble (there were no queues in those days – it was everyone for themselves and inevitably all the males won) I dropped my sixpence through a hole in the floor, so the conductor turfed me off, not believing my story. By this time the tram was only half way to my place of work. What should I do? I walked all the way home in tears wondering where I would get another sixpence from. By that time the "Workman's Return Cheap Fare" time would have finished and the fare would be fourpence. I would only have tuppence for my lunch! When I reached home my mother blew her top and said I must have been mad not to have walked on to work. However, a sixpence was borrowed from our lodgers and off I went again. Reaching work I was told off by the 'Dragon' and stopped half a day's pay. As this was Friday, pay day, I simply had to get to work.

Sometimes during our lunch breaks some of the girls employed on our floor would go to a part of the factory that had no machinery and teach each other the Charleston and the Black Bottom, the Quick Step, the Waltz and the Foxtrot. We had to give this up as the factory rats would come as well and we might have been outnumbered. I was also taught how to make rosettes for horses for the Shire Horse Show (held annually). I think this was the only time that I received any word of praise at the Colditz like place, for the way I made those Rosettes. The 'Dragon' said I could do them better than she could herself. When I left the firm in 1936, no one had learned to make them to her satisfaction other than myself.

During the 1926 General Strike, we of course in the print came out. I was told I would have to take my turn at being a picket. At the age of sixteen I hadn't a clue what that meant. However, I turned up to take my turn and just stood there bored stiff. I had walked all the way from Peckham Rye to Blackfriars for the purpose. When my stint was over my work friend asked me to walk home with her to Islington, so we walked all that way. After a cup of tea and a sandwich I walked back as far as the Elephant and Castle. Luckily I managed to get a lift in a small van with about six others, all bent double, back to Peckham.

We had occasional rises, on birthdays or depending on how you were progressing with your apprenticeship. When you were "Out of Your Time" the final wage was two guineas (£2.2.0) That was that; there were no more rises. On two guineas I stuck for the next nine years until I left to get married. Married women were not allowed to work in the print because of the single girls that were on the dole.

# Shopgirl, Nanny, Waitress, Presser
## Trixie Packe Baker (b. 1909)

Trixie was very backward for her age, having lost much schooling through illness. But although the headmistress wanted her to stay on, she left school at the age of fourteen. An insurance man living in the same block of flats who respected her parents recommended her to a confectioner, who wanted a girl to serve in the shop. She was tall and well mannered, seeming ideal, and so she was engaged. They did not know she was a dunce at maths. Trixie was introduced to the confectioner's wife and little girl. She seemed a sweet child until she got in a temper, when she would punch Trixie in the back.

Trixie mastered the art of breaking toffee in her cupped hand and putting it in a bag or piece of paper if it was for a child. The scales were brass scoops with their weights. A wooden drawer under the counter held copper change in halfpennies and pennies. Behind her on the wall was a shelf with wedges, holding the silver half- crowns, two shilling pieces and shillings for bigger change.

It was a nightmare to Trixie, who couldn't understand any of it. A child came in for a pennyworth of sweets and gave her sixpence. Trixie wrapped the sweets and gave him six pennies change. The lad ran out of the shop as quick as he could go and told all his mates, who before long were back with silver sixpences; a roaring trade was done until the boss found the reason why.

Trixie was then put to do the cleaning of the shop and general chores, which she didn't like and was unhappy. She asked her dad if she could leave; when he said she could, she gave in her notice, but the boss was so annoyed, grumbling at her as she scrubbed the floor. Trixie couldn't control her tears splashing in the bucket. And so ended Trixie's first job.

Trixie's father died shortly after that and she knew she would have to go out to work again. So her sister-in-law made enquiries and heard a lady living in a big house up the hill out in Essex wanted someone to look after her four children and do the housework. The children's ages were between four and eight and the wages were fifteen shillings a week. Trixie was taken on; the woman, whose name was Ada, agreed to give her ten shillings a week.

There were oil lamps to clean, wicks to trim every morning and fireplaces of ashes and cinders, which Trixie spread round the muddy unmade paths. The roads were also unmade, consisting of cart ruts from horse driven sleighs of coal. In the house the carpets were brushed with a hand brush on Trixie's hands and knees and she had to chop up boxes in the cellar for firewood.

In a shed outside there was a billy goat, who had to be taken and tethered in a field near the garden. Every time Trixie bent down to bang in the stake, he lowered his head with its horns. He looked aggressive and prepared to butt her, so she would take to her heels and run, more often than not finding herself in the garden being chased by the goat. Eventually she would land in the field with the goat still in the garden. She would call to grandma, a dear old grandma who dressed the children and did the cooking.

Trixie learned a lesson one day, when helping with the washing up: never to put a hot pudding basin to soak in cold water. She found this out as she watched in horror the bottom of the basin fall out.

The first time Trixie took the children out for a walk, she was nervous, trying to keep them all together. There were no pavements and the two boys, David and Geyus, kept running away. The little girls held her hands. Eventually the boys scrambled up a hedge and were seen no more. Trixie called their names repeatedly, but there was no reply. So, in despair they returned home. Entering the garden gate, they were greeted by the two laughing boys, who had taken a short cut across the fields to be home first.

One day, Trixie was left in charge, as the parents and grandma had to go to London on business. The children were playing nicely after dinner, with crayons and books, when suddenly a flaming piece of coal came down the chimney. Quickly pulling the hearth rug away, Trixie gathered the children together and, pushing them into the garden, told them to stay there until she called them back. With the flaming coal still falling, she shovelled it up into a pail. When the pail was full, she opened the back door and threw it out into the road. Going back, she repeated the performance until no more soot came down and the fire was out. Then after tidying it all up and putting back the mat, she called the children in and made the tea. Trixie told the parents all about it on their return; they must have been grateful to her, knowing what could have happened; with no Fire Brigade and no neighbours to call or telephone, she surely saved the day.

It was not long afterwards that Trixie was told the family was going to live nearer London.

With carpets on the lawn and the general chores that go with moving, the sad day came when she waved them all goodbye. She had grown fond of them in a few months and was sorry to see them go. Trixie's next job was also looking after children. Then she moved back to her family's old flat in Walworth and found a job as a waitress, through the Labour Exchange. But she had to give it up, because the hard work made her ill.

Into the Labour Exchange again, with the familiar smell of carbolic. The queue of women and girls seemed never ending. When eventually her turn came, the assistant said, "I have a vacancy for someone to learn tailoring. Do you think you could do that?" Trixie replied, "I'll have a try at anything."

She took the card with the address on and went to Blackfriars Road. The number was a three storied house in between two lodging houses. She went up a flight of stairs from outside, then a flight of wooden stairs inside, to the first floor, where she could hear the sound of sewing machines. She knocked on the door and a man instantly opened it. She showed him her card and he made way for her to enter a room where girls and women were machining, each busy with their individual tasks. Coming back to the first entry, he said, "You can start at seventeen shillings a week". Trixie was distressed at that; she had been earning twenty-five shillings a week at the restaurant, giving her auntie fifteen out of that.

The man, seeing her agitation, said, "See how you get on. After all, you don't know anything about the work. But if you take to it all right, I will increase it to twenty five shillings in two weeks time."

Trixie agreed to that and said she would start next day. When she arrived, she was introduced to a lady presser who showed her where to attend at the bench opposite her, which was fitted out for pressing. There was a twelve pound iron on a stand to the right of her and a pail of water on a stool beside her. Amy, the presser, was an amiable person and showed her how to change the irons in a gas stove, which was so covered in as to allow just the top of the iron handle to be pulled in and out with the iron holder without getting burned hands. Spreading a coat on the board, Amy showed her how to do the under pressing of seams inside the coat: a 'Dolly' was made from a piece of cloth a few inches wide and tied in the middle after rolling it up sausage-wise. It was dipped into the pail of water, then used to dampen the seams, which were opened by the fingers of the left hand, while you pressed with the iron in the other hand. The iron didn't have to be too hot to scorch. To cool the iron down when needed, a pressing cloth was put through the handle. You held the ends tightly and dipped it in and out swiftly to avoid the steam.

There were eight machinists, four each side of a wooden 'well' which held their work. They were paid piecework: a shilling for a lady's long coat. Consequently Trixie was obliged to press seams as quickly as possible, so as not to keep the other women waiting. She had to throw their parts back to each one to continue making up their coats in rotation. Trixie worked from eight thirty in the morning till six thirty in the evening, with one hour break for midday lunch and ten minutes for tea morning and afternoon, when a girl put the kettle on a gas ring to brew up.

Although the work was hard and tiring, Trixie loved it, except for the time she scalded her hand dipping her iron too far into the pail of boiling water. Her fingers did not work for six months.

Once a year, the boss treated them all to a day's outing by coach either to Southend or Margate, paying for their lunch and tea. They all enjoyed these trips, going on the helter skelter and big dipper in the fair ground and having their photos taken with the presents they won, not to mention the donkey rides. Even the boss's wife joined in paddling in the sea with their dresses tucked into their knickers. Apart from the tea and coffee, they had not a drop to drink, yet they sang at the top of their voices all the way home.

The only bad time in that job was after the Lord Mayor's Show. November 9th was Lord Mayor's Show day, the sign of beginning slack in the rag trade. The girls were put off for a few weeks. They generally went to another firm to make dresses. They returned when the boss got busy again, glad to get back to their old familiar work. When Trixie was put off, she went to the same place the other girls were working. She had made her own dresses on the old machine her mother had used, which had a treadle, so knew she would have to be careful with the power. At ten pence a dress piece work, the firm could afford to let her be careful.

She was given a machine next to one of her friends and shown how to thread. With a dress for a pattern and a bundle of pieces of material, she set about joining them up. Placing two pieces of material together for a seam, she gently put her foot on the treadle. Feeling it slowly moving, she gained courage and, pressing a bit harder, went more quickly until she had finished the seam. The little arm with the cotton threaded that went up and down was on the side of her own machine. On this one it was on the front and she did not notice it until she found she had her hair caught and was fixed. She nudged her pal, saying "Release me, Gert, I've got fixed".

Gertie roared with laughter and called to the others to have a look. They all enjoyed the joke, but when Trixie saw no help was coming she had to cut her hair off herself, making sure none was left to block the machine.

Another time, having put binding round the neck of a dress and while trimming it with her scissors, she was aghast to see she had caught the front of the bodice up and cut a big hole in it. The manageress didn't grumble, but put it aside until she could get another piece of matching material, which meant Trixie waiting to get paid. She earned six shillings the first week and fourteen the second, so she was thankful when the boss sent for her to go back to her old job of pressing. Now Amy taught her to do the top pressing, so she was able to press a coat throughout.

Trixie was twenty and doing overtime till eight o'clock. This was her job until she married and for many years afterwards.

## Escaping the Factory Floor
### Edith Carpenter (b. 1918)

In 1932, as I was almost fourteen, I had to consider what I intended to work at, for I had no choice but to find myself a job. I wanted to do office work because I had heard from my sister Cissie the 'delights' of working in a factory and did not fancy that. I went to Walworth Road, the Careers Office I suppose it would be known as today. They advised me to apply to the Post Office. I sent away for my application form and was told I had to take a test. This was to take place at St Bride's Place in the City, on a Saturday morning.

I had a friend at school, Gladys Stevens, whose mother for many years had a second hand clothes stall in the Lower Marsh. We both went for the test and both passed it. We then had an interview with two people, employed I supposed by the Post Office. They had marked the papers and advised all the successful candidates to wait to be seen; the rest could go home. We were among about eight girls to remain. The others were all grammar school girls and of course older than we were. I don't know how many of them got through the interview, but neither of us did, as we were told some weeks later by a letter sent to our homes. I felt very angry about this failure, for my hopes were so high, having passed the written test. Now I was back to square one, looking for a job.

This time the Labour Exchange gave me a green card and I had to go to see a man at a firm in Southwark Bridge Road. The name of the firm I well remember was Rayments; they made cards, wedding invitation and birthday ones. I was taken on at the weekly wage of ten shillings a week and given a fortnight's trial. During the next two weeks I spent all my time sitting on a high stool, brushing the bits of thin card off the deckled edges of cards that had been stamped out by machine. My next job, when somebody left, I was told, would be to fan out these cards and lightly paint them, so they had a border of a deeper hue. I could not see myself sitting on that stool for the rest of my working life, especially as I never intended to get married myself in those days. So when I was called in the 'office' and asked how I would like to be taken on permanently, I refused and was once more in need of a job.

I went back to the Labour Exchange and was given another green card for yet another factory job. I could see that was to be my future, unless I did something about it, so I found myself a job in a sweet shop in Farringdon Street. That was more to my liking; I enjoyed serving and giving change to the customers. Being the junior, I was expected to act as char as well. That part I did not like, but accepted as part of the job. I had to clean the shop and the steps each morning and the stockroom later in the day. I also had to get the errands for the other two girls who worked there, going across to Hart's the butchers for some cold meat or cheese and the bakers for some rolls for their break. Another part of the job was that sometimes I went to the head office to take some invoices that had arrived with the goods; that I did enjoy, for it made a little outing for me. I stayed with the sweet shop, Lavell's, until I felt it was time I could justifiably leave, not because I did not like the work, but I found I was spending less and less time on the counter and more and more time acting as a sort of housekeeper to the other girls.

I went to Woolworth's in Exmouth Street, just as a Christmas extra. I was asked if I would like to be taken on permanently and was quite happy to be. After the casual work, I now became responsible for a counter. I was to take over the stationery counter. I took a great pride in it and saw it was well stocked up. I tried to keep the customers happy, because if you upset one, they would complain to the manager and out you would go.

The stationery counter consisted of two sections. One was the actual paper, envelopes and writing materials, the other was birthday cards and books. The old ladies who were regular customers would want a card selected and read to them. The cards were all the same price: one penny each. One old lady came in every day without fail for a birthday card; she must have had more friends and relations than anyone else, but good luck to her, for she was very pleasant. Or so I thought, until

138

one day, after reading her card, I noticed her handbag. It was stuffed with half-penny pencils, the little ones that fit into diaries. I was at first sad, thinking she did not know what she was doing, then angry, realising I had been duped, for while I was reading a card, she was pinching my stock. She paid for the card and I got hold of the supervisor and told her what I had seen; she waited until the woman was outside the shop door and then asked her to step back into the rest room at the back of the shop. The poor woman came back into the shop, crossing herself and asking God to forgive her. I felt sorry for her again, until, when they opened her shopping bag, they found she had taken things from every counter in the store, the cunning old bitch. In those days seldom was a shoplifter prosecuted by Woolworths, just warned off the premises and banned from shopping there ever again. That was my first taste of humanity as it really was, for I had been brought up to trust people. I was never as trusting again.

# First Day at Work
## Alf Slater (b. 1927)

September 1941 was an unforgettable and magical milestone for me: I was fourteen and going to work. Staying on at school for any further education or training was at that time almost completely unknown. And so it was off to work I go. Adorned and armed in my over-sized, bright striped, "Four Bob" (twenty pence) long trousers, I proceeded to obtain employment. In 1941 this was a very much easier and a far less daunting task than it is forty plus years later. Many thousands of men and women were in the armed forces, so labour in the various industries, both large and small, was at a premium. But although work was plentiful and reasonably varied, the stability of an apprenticeship training for a trade was difficult to obtain. However, at fourteen, with the prospect of your very own "Few Bob" jingling in your pocket, these things seemed trivial.

During the last week before I left school, I went for interviews to three jobs. The first was at Bloomfield's Garage in Wyndham Road. They offered me fifteen shillings a week. The second was delivering bread on a bike which was so big I'd have needed a ladder to get on the seat. The third was at a small factory set in the railway arches of Crown Street. The name was John Pinches and Son. They made wire trays, for grilling and steaming food, and umbrella shaped trainers for roses. Mr Brock, the manager, informed me that there was a vacancy for a boy in the wire shop and that my wages would be one pound and threepence a week.

My hours of work were eight until six, with an hour off for dinner – it was always called a dinner hour; this made a working week of 45 hours. It was later reduced to 43½ hours.

On that first visit, the manager took me along to the foreman, a small man who was wearing riding breeches; he must have sensed my thoughts, because the first

139

words he said were, "Don't frown lad; these are for my bike".

"Oh dear", I thought, "what a start!"

"Has Mr Brock told you about your money and hours?"

"Yes", I replied.

"OK then, see you Monday; I'll tell you what's to be done then."

As I turned to go, he said, "Remember it's your first day; don't be late.' Then with a little smile, he added, "By the way, I like your long trousers, very colourful! Cheerio!" It had all happened in fifteen minutes – just a quarter of an hour to cross the threshhold that divides school from work.

On the Monday morning, my mother woke me at seven o'clock. I dressed and went into the kitchen. On the table was a large plate of steaming Quaker Oats. "Get that down yer – it'll make yer feel like a fighting cock," she said. There was also a cup and a parcel of sandwiches to take to work. It was then that the finality of it all really got to me. I suddenly felt sick with fear of the unknown. I felt anything but elated and grown-up – certainly not a "fighting cock".

I arrived at work at ten minutes to eight and stood by the foreman's office waiting for him to appear. The rest of the men were beginning to arrive. Some were only a couple of years older than myself. There were about eight. Everyone gave me a nod or a wave. That was a reassuring sign, I can tell you. One of them came over to me and said, "Hello, kid. My name's Monty, yeah, that's right – same name as that general bloke in the desert". Monty went on, "Old Becky's late this morning. 'E 'as to bike it from Welling, yer know. Must've 'ad an 'old up somewhere. 'E's gonna be well pleased when 'e comes in – it's piddling cats and dogs outside". As he turned to walk away he said, "'Ere, it's yer first day, ain't it?"

"Yes", I replied.

"Don't worry, Cocker," he said. "You'll be all right". And with a smile he added, "Let's 'ope 'is breeches ain't shrunk".

After what seemed an eternity, Mr Beck the foreman appeared in the doorway. "Becky" had arrived. He had a cycling cape that went below his knees and an enormous pointed rain-hat that almost covered his face. As he walked into the room, he showered water everywhere.

"'Allo there, submarine leaking was it?" someone remarked.

"Nah, I reckon 'is bike must've sank", was the reply.

I don't know how I kept a straight face, but being my first day I thought it best not to laugh. Becky pretended not to notice, but then he started muttering loud enough for everyone to hear: "They've closed the bleedin' roads to mend the 'oles. I've 'ad ter come all round the bloody 'ouses. Fancy doin' that when it's pissin' down with rain". As he got to his office door, he turned and added, "So I don't want to 'ear any more remarks from you lot about leaking subs or sinking bikes."

"Oh dear", I thought. "This don't seem such a good start to my first day". But as he went into his office he had a little smile, so perhaps he wasn't such a bad bloke after all. "Won't be long lad. Be with you in a minute", he said. I thought he hadn't noticed me.

After a while he emerged and remarked, "Right, here we go. Let's start telling you your job and your duties". He informed me that my first job every morning was light a fire in the stove. This was a round cast iron compund, approximately eighteen inches in diameter and three feet high. There was an opening in the top into which you fed the fuel. Coke was the medium of fuel for this type of fireburner. Although coal and coke were rationed, a small factory such as this was able to obtain a fair ration. The fire's main function was to supply heating during the winter. The days of efficient and automatic central heating in workplaces were some years away.

When the fire was going, I had to put a large kettle of water on the stove for the tea break at ten o'clock. This was repeated at two o'clock for the tea break at four o'clock. I kept a watchful eye on the fire, because I remembered the foreman saying, "Woe betide you if the lads don't get their tea on time".

There was no official time allowed for tea breaks. You made your tea and carried on working. The 'Factory Act Ruling' at that time stated that a break should only be taken after five hours. This was the reason that dinner hours were from one until two during the course of a nine hour day. I learned this many years later. On this particular day my only thought was to have the kettle boiling on time.

After the tea and ten the foreman beckoned me and handed me a tin box. "Put this on the stove, lad", he said. "Handle it very carefully – there's a rice pudding inside. I want it ready for my dinner hour".

During the year that I spent at this job before I left to take up a training for my present trade, the same procedure happened. The tin box appeared with the inevitable rice pudding every day. How he ever biked it from Welling every day with all that rice pudding inside him is a mystery to me. The lads at the firm reckoned that he had his own private 'rice field'.

Between the kettles and the rice pudding, the remainder of my first day was spent in getting acquainted with the productive nature of my employment. I was informed that it was in my interest to learn quickly, because this firm, I was informed, operated an incentive to earn a few shillings extra. It was called 'piecework time system'. This was all too much for me to grasp on my first day. What it meant in fact was this: you were given a certain amount of items to be completed in a given time. If you completed in the given time, the target time it was called, a few shillings extra would be added to your wages. On looking back at such an ingenious system, I see a very uneven contest. I well remember that in the following few months my only reward was sweat, bruised fingers and frustration. My only compensation was my growing ability with the stove, kettle and the ever present rice pudding.

At five minutes to six Mr Beck came out of his office, glanced at the clock and said, "Right lads, clear up and go home". He looked at me and added, "Well done, youngster. See you tomorrow – don't be late!" And so ended my momentous first day at my first job – but not quite. I hurried home, told my mother most of the events of the day, had my tea and then asked her to lend me fourpence until Friday. I was going to the Savoy to see that new film, "The Flying Tigers". It was an 'A' film, which meant that no one under the age of sixteen should be admitted without an adult. But having just finished my first day at work, I wanted to try out my new found manhood. I marched up to the paybox, hands in my pockets, displaying my long trousers, produced my money, got my ticket and boldly marched in . . . The day was complete.

# Chapter Eight
# Monkeys' Parade, Courting
# and Marriage

## Monkeys' Parade
### Lil Blore (b. 1905)

When I was about 16, every weekend my friend and I would go for long walks to Red Post Hill. It was all country then. All the young boys would stand along the top – Monkeys' Parade they called it. My friend, who worked at a milliner's, had a pretty black straw hat which she paid 1/6d for. I would have liked one too but had only a faded yellow straw one. So I painted it black with Brunswick blacking, which my mother used to black the grates. It smelled awful, so we put it outside to let the smell go. Then we saw some dyed chicken wings – blue – in a shop and we bought two - 2/6d each. I had three shillings pocket money each week from the sixteen shillings I had in wages. Anyway, two boys took my friend and me to the Golden Dome (now the International Stores). We sat between the two boys and after a while one of them said, "There's a horrible smell – what can it be?"

My friend began to giggle and after a while she told them it was my hat. Everyone laughed their heads off except me. I was so ashamed. I would never go out with those boys again.

After that I made my own hats: a wire frame which cost 1/6d; a quarter of a yard of black lace for the crown and brim; and a red rose, which I used to sew in the side. They were called "Valencia" hats.

## Boy Meets Girl
### Ben Moakes (b. 1904)

It was October 1921. I was minding my father's catsmeat stall in Waterloo Street, as it was then called, by Camberwell Green. I was now reconciled to the fact that this was how I was to earn my living.

Fifteen months previously, at the age of sixteen, I had left the fifth form of Wilson's Grammar School. In parting, my Form Master, Mr Wiggett, had said, "Work is scarce. If the only job you can get is sweeping floors, be sure to sweep

*The Moakes family's catsmeat stall*

them cleaner than they have ever been swept before." Only two jobs had been offered me. One was as pupil teacher at a local school. I rejected this because I saw no prospect of children in my own neighbourhood showing me any respect; if I tried to enforce discipline it would result in quarrels with their parents. The second offer was by an Insurance Company, who would pay me £1 a week for a probationary period of six months. If suitable, I would be retained at the regular rate of pay. Dad told me to turn this down. He visualised a stream of youngsters getting the low pay for six months – and then being classed as unsuitable, making way for more cheap labour. He considered I could earn £3 a week with a catsmeat stall.

For a short time I had one at the junction of Camberwell New Road and Station Road. What little I earned was from Dad's own customers in that area, buying from me to save themselves a journey. So we gave it up.

Next I had a try at Greenwich, just off Trafalgar Road. After two weeks I pushed the barrow back to Camberwell, for on that final day I had only taken one penny. So I came back to looking after Dad's stall, as my elder brother had done before he enlisted in the army.

Now, on this October day, my friend Stanley Baxter, nicknamed "Stand Back" was chatting to me. We were Rover Scouts in "Blackie's Own" Troop, the 112th South London. Stan was a good-looking chap with curly hair and a cheeky grin, attractive to girls, and as the young ladies were coming home from local factories, he was enjoying himself making flirtatious remarks to them. None took offence and many smiled back. I felt a bit left out, as I was far too shy to make any approach to a strange girl. However, I summoned up my courage as a pretty girl with dark, curly hair approached. I greeted her with some trivial, banal remark. She blushed, smiled and murmured something before continuing homeward.

On subsequent days, emboldened by this first success, I got into conversation with her. I learned that her name was Lizzie Reynolds. Both her parents had died and she lived with an aunt, uncle and cousins. Lizzie was usually accompanied by her friend, Alice, who worked with her at the Melhuish factory, packing bags of flour for retail sale in shops. I also discovered that Lizzie was five months younger than me, whilst Alice was one day older. Consequently, her reply to any flippant remark of mine was "Don't sauce your elders!"

It wasn't long before I asked Lizzie if she would go out with me. To my great joy she consented and we made a date for the following Sunday.

But when Sunday came I was despondent. I had been wearing my only suit every day at the stall. It had become quite greasy and no matter how hard I brushed it, the coat looked terrible. I was all right for trousers. George Cocks, who lived opposite, had bought his son Johnny a blue serge suit with an extra pair of trousers some time previously, but Johnny had grown rapidly and the spare trousers wouldn't fit him now. Dad paid George thirty bob for the trousers and waistcoat, neither having been worn. But I was wearing them now, standing in the back yard, hopelessly brushing away, wondering how Lizzie would feel if I didn't show up for our very first date.

Our little house was a two up, two down type, with the passage running direct through it from front to back door. I heard a man's voice at the street door calling down the passage, "Missus, have you got a boy this coat will fit?"

I nearly knocked Mum over in my rush to see the coat. It was blue serge! I tried it on. It fitted me well.

"How much?" Mum asked.

"I'll take half-a-crown", the man replied.

He received it immediately. Mum gave me a little smile. "God's good" she said. "He don't come himself, but he sends someone."

So, feeling like Beau Brummel, I set off to keep my engagement. But I got another upset: Alice was with Lizzie. At this time Dad used to give me two shillings and sixpence a week pocket money, so I was never very flush. Could I manage to pay for three seats at the pictures? Only the cheapest ones.

Lizzie took my arm. I felt great again. I stopped at Charlie Lettsom's shop and bought some Milk Tray chocolates. I offered them to Lizzie and was stunned when she took not just one chocolate, but the whole packet. Never having taken a girl out before, I was unaware of the correct procedure between a lady and her escort.

*Ben and Lizzie*

*The bandstand, Peckham Rye*

"How can I get rid of Alice?" I puzzled, but dared not be rude to her, so we chatted away gaily as we made for the Grand Hall in Camberwell New Road.

There were queues when we arrived. This gave me a breathing space. My pocket held three shillings and sixpence. The seats would be one and threepence each.

"I don't like lining up outside a cinema," I exclaimed. "Everybody watches you. Let's go for a little walk, then when we come back we will be able to go straight in."

The girls didn't disagree, so I took them up Warner Road and zig-zagged about till we got past Loughborough Junction.

"We'll make our way back now," I said. "Which way do we go?"

I was lucky, they had no idea of the way. So I worked around to Myatts Fields, Knatchbull Road, Station Road and eventually reached the Grand Hall at about nine fifteen. We decided unanimously that it wasn't worth going into the cinema when the programme was half over, so I escorted them to a café for a cup of tea and cake, amply covered by my three and sixpence.

We shook hands demurely and said goodnight. The next time I took Lizzie out we were alone. Alice didn't like playing gooseberry and found other things to do.

My Dad bought the goodwill of a catsmeat round from an elderly man who was retiring, so I got a reasonable wage, instead of just having pocket money. Lizzie and I fell deeply in love and saved hard to get married. But in 1925 the E.W. Douglas motorcycle came on the market, in its time the last word in modern machines. I fell in love with this too and blued our savings on acquiring one. The bike cost £42 and the sidecar £17. Afterwards we saved all the harder. We were finally married at St. George's Church, Wells Street (Way) on Easter Day, April 17, 1927.

## Girl Meets Boy
## Phyl Hall (b. 1910)

When I was sixteen my mother had another baby, a boy this time. I felt very unhappy about this as I had done nothing but look after babies ever since I could remember. I knew it would mean that I would still have to be in by 8.30 in the evening so that my parents could go along to the pub whilst I looked after the younger children.

If the weather was nice, when my parents went off to the pub on a Sunday night, I was allowed to stay out a little longer if I took my sisters with me. On one occasion when I did this, I met my friend Winnie at the Bandstand on Peckham Rye. The look of dismay on her face was something to be seen. "Oh! Why do you have to bring your blooming kids with you every time we go to the bandstand?" she cried. "We will never 'get off' while you bring them!"

147

What a disaster this turned out to be! We sorted out some boys we thought would be "likely lads". After some chat with them, they grabbed hold of the pushchair holding my small sister and ran off. Suddenly the pushchair tipped up, throwing my sister out and was my face red – she had no knickers on! That was the last time Winnie met me at the bandstand plus two kids.

As I was now a working girl I felt that I should have the privilege of staying out a bit later when I went out with my friends. I was always rather timid and shy and always did as my parents told me, until one day my friend that I had had from my schooldays said, "You must be mad to always get in by 8.30. Why don't you stay out until about 10 o'clock and see what happens?"

This I did. When I came home, my father, who would never miss going to the pub, was waiting at the gate for me; he started bawling and hitting me, but I actually had enough courage to answer him back. I told him I was now grown up and no longer a schoolchild and as I paid my weekly earnings into the household I was entitled to some privileges. After some arguments with my parents I was allowed to stay out until ten o'clock.

My friends and I had rounds of parties, where of course we looked for boy friends. At one of the parties I went to I met the boy who was to become my future husband. For me that was when my life began. I was twenty years of age and it was 1930. My boy friend took me out to dances, dinner dances, days at the seaside; he bought me the best seats at the cinema and theatres, boxes of chocolates, presents of jewellery. We went to parties nearly every weekend, because he could play the piano and the drums and was always in demand at parties.

Having met in October 1930, we were both 21 in the February of 1931. My boy friend, whom we called "My young man" in those days, decided we would like to go away on holiday together. Cliftonville, near Margate, was our choice. The problem was would my parents allow me to go away with him? After a lot of persuasion they said yes. We booked some seats on a coach for 12/6d return to Cliftonville and two rooms at a boarding house. A letter had to be shown to my parents as proof we did indeed have two separate rooms.

Our boarding house charge would be two guineas each for full board, which included four good meals a day. It was really a fantastic holiday; our fellow boarders were a very jolly crowd. In the evenings we would all go to the Cliff Café, which was really a dance hall, one of a complex of other dance halls. I think the total cost of that holiday was £10 for the two of us.

After about a year courting we decided to get engaged, but it took another five years to save up £120, enough to get married on, just about, in 1936. My mother did not exactly encourage us as she could see an end to my weekly contribution to the family's expenses.

We managed to get most of the essential items, at least, essential in those days: a three-piece suite, a bedroom suite and a dining room suite; each room was covered in lino – no wall-to-wall carpeting in the Thirties – with just a hearth-rug at each fireplace. We considered ourselves lucky to be able to rent a three-roomed flat for eighteen shillings per week. I had to leave my work in the print, as married women were not allowed to work because of the "means test" resulting from the unemployment situation at that time.

I had a lovely wedding. My deaf sister, who was trained by Norman Hartnell, the Queen Mother's dressmaker, made my dress in ivory satin and the four bridesmaids' dresses in floral pink voile. About forty people came to the wedding. My mother, aunts and I did the catering and the reception was held at my parents' house. My father had made the garden look very pretty and adorned it with floodlights and fairy lights.

We went away the next morning for our honeymoon to Shanklin, Isle of Wight. My husband, who worked as an engineer at the Old Kent Road Bus Garage, had a take-home pay of £3.18.0. We decided that we could afford to get a wireless on the hire purchase for 1/9d per week. My husband, being such a keen piano player, could not be without a piano for long, so we decided to get one on hire purchase too. The cost was £35, which included the piano stool – all straight from the factory. This was the basic price; the interest had to be added to this. We started paying in 1937 and, what with missing a few payments when we were short of cash and the war coming along, we made the final payment in 1940. We sold it when TV came on the scene, for £20.

## The Only Boyfriend I Ever Had
## Ada Bennett (b. 1901)

My stepsister went to the South London Palace one Saturday evening with a friend and met two young men. My stepmother, always ready for new faces, invited them in. After then one, whose name was Frank, was a constant visitor. It was me he came to see. I was nearly fifteen and he was just turned seventeen. He took me to Southend for a day; that was the first time I saw the sea. His name for me was "Cinders". We found out that we had both been at Hanwell School, a boarding school for homeless children (see my piece in Chapter 3).

When the war ended, my father, who was in the army, was in hospital with complications. He was sent home in March 1919, but died six weeks later. My stepmother received his gratuity money and all his back pay. She put ten shillings on the table and told me to get out. I left home on my eighteenth birthday with just what I stood up in. She would not let me take anything with me. I do not know what I would have done without Frank's help. I made my home with my mother's sister. She was a widow with four children.

Frank was the only boy friend I ever had. We got engaged at Christmas, 1920, and married on Christmas Day (a Sunday), 1921.

We managed to get two rooms with the help of a friend and bought two rooms of furniture for 46 guineas. It was advertised as a complete home. It was all we needed at the time. I found out later that our landlady had known my family and had attended my mother's funeral. She was very good to us and treated us just like her own family. She was with me when my two children were born.


## Trixie and Jack
### Trixie Packe Baker (b. 1908)

In the summer evenings when Trixie was in her early teens, she would skate round the streets on roller skates her brother gave her, sometimes clinging to the boys' bikes. Dad called her "Legs and Wings" as her arms and legs went flying.

Boy friends called for her, but she wasn't interested.

One very nice boy couldn't resist calling for her to go out with him. She asked her brother to tell him firmly that she didn't want to. He did not call again.

Fred, her brother, was courting a girl who lived in the same street and it was understood Trixie would ask her anything she wanted to know personally, which she did, when they met to go to the Baths once a week. Some things she found too embarassing to ask about, but her mother's sister, Auntie Polly, who lived upstairs on the next landing, was jolly and forthright and left nothing to the imagination. She told her all she wanted to know and more.

Trixie learned to play the piano by ear and one party her Auntie gave was such a success, it lasted well into the night. Auntie Polly went to bed leaving the guests to their dancing, eventually to pair off. Trixie was alone.

She thought of the friend of her cousin's who had asked her to go out with him, when she wasn't interested. Now she was having second thoughts. He would be company, she mused, so she asked her cousin if he would tell his friend she would like to see him.

The next day he called on her and she said, "I will go out with you if you still want me to." Then she added hastily, "But I don't love you."

"That's all right by me. I'm only too pleased you will go out with me," Jack answered.

From then on they went for walks in the evenings from the Elephant and Castle to either Waterloo Bridge, London Bridge or Blackfriars, along the Embankment beside the River Thames, then home over any one of the other bridges to say goodnight at the block entrance in Sayer Street, where Trixie lived. Jack went round to Lion Street, where he lived with his mum and dad, six brothers and three sisters, on the top floor. He was eighteen at this time and Trixie seventeen.

One day, Trixie's brother who was now married with a baby girl and also living

in the same block of flats, said to her, "Why don't you buy a tandem? You would enjoy cycling. I could order one to suit your requirements and I would come out with you on long runs to set the pace." Brother Fred understood these things, having been in the Cycling Corps in the Army.

Trixie knew Jack wouldn't be able to afford it. Although he had won a scholarship at school and went to the Borough Polytechinc, he had had to leave school at sixteen and get the first job he could, to help his mother. But after all, Trixie would get the benefit, so she thought nothing of drawing the money out of her Post Office Savings book and Fred was able to get a very worthwhile tandem, with the best components, for £18. Weekends would see them starting out at midnight, with Brother Fred on his solo bike setting the pace through towns and villages, stopping occasionally at a wayside café for a cup of tea. They always took flasks of tea and sandwiches to eat at their destination, which was either Brighton, Worthing or Bognor, being the end of the least hilly routes to the South Coast. The sight of the early sunrise over the Downs was something never to be forgotten. They would make their way to their destination, only to sink on the lonely beach about six o'clock in the morning and fall fast asleep.

They usually started back in the early afternoon to avoid the traffic, arriving home about seven o'clock.

Fred didn't always go with them, but neither Trixie nor Jack were amorous. The weeks and months rolled away; in fact four years passed, until one day, while sitting in Kennington Park, Jack asked Trixie if she would marry him. She agreed, although she felt she still didn't love him, but they were good company.

They went along to a jewellers in London Road; Trixie went inside and chose a diamond ring, while Jack waited outside. They were engaged for another four years.

During this time, Trixie found a job she really liked (after four previous ones). She settled down to be a Tailor Presser, with twelve pound irons.

Jack's firm closed down and he was out of work for six months, after which he

151

had his dole money stopped and couldn't pay his mother. They then realised she was managing without his money and decided to get married. Jack got another job soon after, as a packer in a clothing warehouse in the City.

Trixie didn't like the idea of hire purchase, so was relieved and thankful when friends of Jack's mum in the furniture trade let them have their furniture at cost price and a flat upstairs in their house at Clapham Common.

Trixie made her wedding dress in white satin and wanted two small bridesmaids in pale yellow to carry primroses and two older girls to carry daffodils in pale green dresses. But, although she went in stores all over the West End, she couldn't get the right colours until she went down East Street and got just the right colours she wanted in a shop with a stall outside.

Trixie wore her mother's veil, which luckily waited until after the ceremony before falling to pieces. While they were having their photos taken outside the church in New Kent Road, a coach load of fellows going to a football match called out, amid laughter from everyone, "Don't do it!"

Everyone crossed over the road to Sayer Street and Auntie Polly's for a buffet which Trixie had prepared earlier. The flat was full of people chatting merrily – friends and relatives who hadn't met for years, sitting on beds or standing in the hall. All Trixie's girls from work came, even the boss, so she asked him if he would cut the wedding cake to make it go further. Trixie was wondering if there were enough refreshments, when someone remembered it was dinner time and Palm Sunday. She had chosen that day because her parents were married then, but later on, when she realised the religious meaning, she wished she had chosen Easter Sunday.

The wedding had been early and people were hanging about. If only someone had guided them to go away for the weekend, it would have been less embarassing and everyone would have left earlier. As it was, Trixie and Jack had to go to work the next day; had they chosen Easter they would have had the Bank Holiday off.


# How? What? When? Why?
## Alf Slater (b. 1927)

How? . . . What? . . . When . . . And Why? The reply to these basic questions left you thinking, "I wonder . . . I wonder . . . I wonder . . ." This just about summed up the extent of sex education for the young person forty years ago.

In the 1980's the subject of sex is commonplace – in newpapers, books, magazines, films, the supply of information, and in some instances misinformation, seems endless. But for parents it is no easy task to explain in detail this very important fact of life. I know, because I am a parent. Yet at least parents strive, even if they are still reluctant, to impart knowledge; and any information that is given is not bound up in the mumbo-jumbo that I had to endure during my early teens and growing-up period in the 1940's.

At that time it was oh, so very much different. The subject of sex was completely and absolutely taboo. Any enquiry by the young and inquisitive mind was treated as if you had asked for details of the Official Secrets Act. The verbal response and occasionally the physical one, could often deter you from any further enquiry in that direction. But usually the accompanying "Hmm's", "Er's" and "Arrh's" along with the shuffling of feet and nervous coughs were enough to make you feel guilty, apologetic and with a "Sorry I asked" kind of feeling. The one glimmer of hopeful information – after the shocked parent had recovered – was the promise to tell you of the "Birds and Bees" and of "Babies and Gooseberry Trees". What a mystery! No wonder we were sorry we had asked.

To add to this continual reference to the "Birds and Bees" and babies being found under a "Gooseberry Tree", a further complication arose about this sweet mystery of life. My mate informed me one day that his mother had told him in response to his enquiry as to how he was born that she had eaten some new bread and then went into the scullery to do her washing and there he was, perched on top of the copper. So now I had a further question to ask. Why had they changed places? . . . From being found under a "Gooseberry Tree" they were now on top of the copper. "Was it boiling at the time?" I asked. "Dunno, she didn't say", he replied. Then he added, "But she did say I was crying."

The list of perplexing wonder was beginning to lengthen. It now seemed that we had to include the baker, the boiling copper and the possibility that we were all born with burnt bums. To attempt to comprehend all this and then to try and find a connection between new bread, sculleries, scalded bottoms and washing days was all too much for our young minds to assimilate at that time – especially in relation to the facts of life.

I then thought of an ingenious plan in an effort to obtain some snippets of information: I would sit in the corner of the room, with my head buried in "Film Fun", pretending to be engrossed with "Our Gang". My mother and married sister would be talking: "What about that 'Molly Bloggs' then?" my mother would say.

"Yes I know, she was with this bloke and . . ."

My whirling ears suddenly lost the sound of my sister's reply. I realised I had been tumbled; my cover was blown, my intention "sussed". That old grown-up trick of moving the lips without any sound was being used. I knew exactly what would happen when sound returned: "Alfie, sling yer 'ook, me and yer sister's talkin' ".

"Bloody clever, these parents," I thought. "They 'orter be in the Secret Service."

After hearing so much about "The Birds and Bees", the desperate thought

153

even entered my head as to whether they could tell me anything, because, try as I may, I could only think of a gooseberry bush as something that went with pie and custard.

It was like this till I started work. Then suddenly a whole new image was portrayed. My further education in the subject of sex changed dramatically. This new dimension of misguided learning was now assaulting my ears with stories of "Man and Woman" . . . "Letters from France" . . . "Pudding Clubs" . . . and "Be Careful". These are just a few of the printable references; some of the more colourful and illuminating stories are best left to the imagination.

With all this new-found information I began to get an increasing awareness of the subject. Also, the lip-reading conversations at home about Molly Bloggs and the blokes had now progressed to a low sound that nearly reached my ears when I was present. And I wasn't told to "Sling yer 'ook, we're talking." They were aware that I was at work and that the fog of the unknown was becoming the mist of the uncertain.

But there were still many moments of uncertainty, like the day that one of the blokes came to work with a face as long as a kite – in other words, completely fed-up with himself.

"What's wrong?" I asked.

"My wife's having a baby and I don't know how it happened," he replied.

"Did she eat a lot of new bread then?" I asked quite seriously. His uncontrolled laughter still haunts me. It made his day brighter, but mine continued with a puzzled frown, because when the laughter stopped he said, "Na' it's George the barber's fault – he never had any French fings left. The crisp tin on the top shelf was empty and now she's in the club."

"What French fings?" I asked.

"Them letters," he replied.

No wonder things were difficult to understand; I couldn't speak a word of French, so how could I read a letter? It may have been confusing, but I had to ask, "Does ol' George run a club then, 'cos I've never seen any women in there?"

He was laughing again . . . "Don't yer know anyfing about the birds and bees?" he said.

I suddenly thought of something. " 'Ere", I said. "There's a bloke down the Lane with a cap and white coat. 'E calls 'isself the ol' firm. Is 'e anyfing to do with them French fings?"

He laughed and replied, "Yeh, that's right, stands near the bloke that sells 'orseradish." Then he roared with laughter and added "Be funny if they got 'em mixed up wouldn't it? But yer learnin' son, ain't yer?"

# Chapter Nine
# The Second World War, 1939-45

## The Phoney War
## Alf Slater (b. 1927)

As I began to prepare for my further elevation to the top floor at school, the "Big Boys" as it was known, the spectre of war was approaching. A few strange faces began to appear amongst us at the school. They could speak very little English and wore different clothes, without any patches. One of them even had leather trousers. The Headmaster told us to be kind to them; "They are refugees and have come to this country to escape from the Germans," he said. The threat of the cane or a twisted ear was never needed to achieve the silence that followed as the Headmaster went on, "There is the possibility that this country will be at war. London may be bombed. Many of you will be evacuated into the country for your own safety". In his slow and deliberate way he continued, "Should this occur, school will probably be suspended for a little time if there are not enough teachers or pupils available".

He had stopped talking, but the words were still booming around like an echo "War" . . . "London Bombed" . . . "Evacuated away from home" . . . "School Suspended" . . . They remained on the treadmill of thought within my mind. As I looked around the hall at the teachers who were present, I realised how serious the situation was. The little eccentric mannerisms that some of them had for stern situations seemed to be very much in evidence: the headmaster, Mr Mortleman, was continually pulling at his stiffly starched collar; Mr Flynn, our music teacher, had his hands behind his back and was staring at the ceiling, just like when we hit a wrong note at choir practice; Mr Dillon had his glasses at the end of his nose, hands clasped in front, and was slowly bending his knees – the school's 'Hit Man' was mentally giving six of the best to whoever was responsible for this. If war came and they went away I would miss them; they weren't so bad after all. One thing I was certain about though – I was not going to be evacuated.

And so it happened . . . On Sunday September the third, nineteen thirty nine, just before we were due back at school from the summer holidays, war was declared. I returned to find that many of my friends and a number of the teachers had already been evacuated to Devon. It was all very much different; so much had happened in a short space of time. The school was half empty and strangely quiet. In the classrooms on the ground floor, brown paper was stuck on the windows to stop flying glass if any bombs dropped close by. Bags of sand were piled against the wall for added protection. The most important item that you brought with you each day was your gas mask.

Although there were a number of new faces at the school, some of the teachers that I knew were still there. Mr Mortleman and his starched collar was still our headmaster. Miss Maynard was as always busily engaged everywhere, with that ever-lasting frown, and the other teacher I was more than glad to see was Mr Irving. He was our sports master, my big hero ever since one of the boys told me that he'd had a trial for Everton. Whether it was true or not I didn't care; he was a great footballer and in the year before the war had started had made St. Joseph's one of the best school teams in South London.

*A South London school football team*

As the weeks and months progressed, school began to settle into something like its normal routine. As far as we were concerned in London, the war as yet was having little effect. The weather was quite good and I almost began to envy some of my mates that had been evacuated to the green fields of Devon. If it hadn't been for the sandbags, the policemen with their tin hats on and the blacked-out streets at night, you wouldn't have known there was a war. I remember my elder brother saying to my Mum: "They're calling this the 'Phoney War' and they think it will be over by Christmas . . . !"

Well, Christmas came and went; we even had a school party, but had to supply our own food because of the rationing. Mr Irving formed a team and we played a few matches against some other schools. Back playing school football – that had to be normal. Some of the girls – because we were now a mixed school – were kept busy knitting balaclava hats to send to our troops in France.

But suddenly it all changed. Our troops were sent towards the sea in France; the history and legend of Dunkirk were born. There was talk of 'invasion', 'Home

Guards', 'fighting in the streets'. There were speeches from Mr Churchill (our new Prime Minister) and German propaganda from "Lord Haw Haw". It was all becoming very confusing and tense. Through all this, school was still functioning as normally as possible; my only immediate problem was to get there on time and keep a lily-white palm unmarked by the teacher's cane; once I was there, especially on time, I was a model prisoner and gave no trouble.

Then one Saturday afternoon when I was looking forward to my twelfth birthday and hoping I would get a new pair of football boots, the sirens sounded and the bombers appeared. The Blitz on London, bringing the fear and horror of real war, had begun.


# The Blitz
## Alf Slater (b. 1927)

The long mournful one-note sound of the siren signalled the all clear. I helped my mother to gather our pillows and blankets together. As we emerged from the air-raid shelter, it was just beginning to get light. Another dusk to dawn air-raid on London had ceased, at least for the hours that separated day from night.

As we wearily climbed the stairs to our flat on the second floor of Evelina Mansions in New Church Road, I heard my mother say, "Thank God that's over. What a night!"

We had just spent almost eleven hours in that shelter; the Blitz on London was growing in intensity.

What a night it had certainly been, because it was one of the nights during the Blitz when I experienced real fear and terror. The bombers had droned overhead for most of the night and there was a constant piercing whistle as the bombs came down. "Don't worry," said one of the men, "The longer you hear the whistle, the further away they are". He went on to add, "sounds as if the docks are copping it, poor sods".

Although we were some couple of miles or so from the docks, the air gradually became filled with a mixture of burning and spent cordite from the exploding shells of our own Ack-Ack guns, which were firing in an attempt to break up the formation of bombers.

About one o'clock in the morning there was a lull. I went with some of the men to the top of our flats to have a look – after all, I was thirteen and having no father I was my mother's protector, so I thought. We were confronted with a sea of flames that seemed to stretch from one end of London to the other. Huge flames were leaping and heaving a mountainous blanket of sparks high into the night. As we gazed at this man-made incandescent nightmare, we heard the steady heavy sound of more aircraft approaching. Fingers of light from our searchlights were hopefully probing the sky; then the Ack-Ack guns were once again attempting to repel the ceaseless horde. The sound of the planes became loud and menacing like a giant heavily laden lorry climbing a steep hill. The lull had ended; the respite was brief and abrupt. Fear was returning.

"Here come the big boys. They're well loaded by the sound of 'em", said a man. "Might as well stay a while – we know where they're going; they won't waste any round 'ere", he added.

I remember how quiet the men were. Whatever they were thinking I will never know, but my thoughts were full of awe and fearful fascination. The bombers roared overhead. The cauldron of flame from the docks propelled them towards the enticing core of its fury. As the bombs exploded deep in its flaming midriff, the flames erupted with renewed force. Every so often a sudden surge would change colour and a huge belt of swirling black smoke would emerge. This told us that oil bombs were being used to fuel the furnace.

As the fear within me progressed, I had the urge to look no more. "I'm going back", I said. As I went back to the shelter, my young mind was besieged with the hell of a hundred nightmares . . . surely nothing would stop that fire; it would roll on and on and engulf us all – perhaps the whole of London would be charred remains in a couple of hours . . . perhaps it might even keep going all over the country. As I sat down beside my mother in the shelter, I could hear the clanging of bells from the fire engines racing through the streets, accompanied no doubt by ambulances and rescue services. I began to think again: if they drained every ocean in the world it would not stop that rolling tide of flame. As I leaned back against the wall of the shelter, I was certain that it was getting warm . . . Was the fire that close already? My mother was speaking to me, but I don't remember a word – my mind was a riot of fear and illogical thoughts.

I must have dozed off to sleep, because the next thing I remember was my mother saying, "Come on, it's over. Get the pillows and blankets together; let's get upstairs". Another night of the Blitz had ended.

The flats where we lived were built in 1900 by a charitable trust called 'The Four Per Cent Industrial Dwellings'. They consisted of four blocks of twenty-four flats. Each block had a shelter erected for them. The one for our block was in the area of the basement, just below the level of the street. It was a concrete structure measuring approximately eight feet wide by about twenty feet long and six feet high. There were three long wooden forms to sit on, two small cubicles for toilets – not the flushing kind, just an old tin drum – and an iron ladder, which went to the square iron escape hatch at the opposite end to the entrance. It is not surprising, therefore, that the majority of the people in the ground and basement flats preferred to take their chance in their homes or take a trip down the tube. As the hours spent in the shelter grew longer at night, the need for sleep became important. One of the forms was taken out to enable some of the older people and children to lay on the floor. The rest of the people wrapped themselves in blankets and attempted to sleep on the remaining two wooden forms. Lack of sleep became a way of life.

After all these years, as I write this, I can view these people as something special in my mind. Their courage and resilience is an inspiration, especially that which they showed on another night, the one when we heard no whistle from the bomb and I thought the shelter was to be my tomb.

I do not remember exactly what night it was. It was possibly another Saturday, because I do remember that we had been singing – and this usually happened on Saturday nights because, bombs or no bombs, the men would always have a couple of pints, if beer was available, and get us singing. We could hear the menacing growl of the bombers approaching and the sporadic bangs of our own guns, but we were singing and felt happy. We raised our voices and attempted to compete. The heavy throbbing of the engines came very loud and directly over-head – our singing was beginning to falter. I think we all sensed that this could be something different.

Everything happened so quickly, in just a few seconds . . . that's all the time it takes. The first whistle was short and the explosion stung our ears . . That was close!

"Our singing wasn't that bad, was it?" someone remarked.

The next one produced much the same effect, but the light appeared to dance a crazier pattern. We then had what I can only describe as a huge rush of wind. A peculiar type of pressure seemed to invade the shelter; the sensation was like sitting in a train and entering a tunnel at high speed. A minute part of a second elapsed . . . that immeasurable time that separates carnage from commonsense. I was transfixed with terror as the frightening aftermath began to manifest itself.

There was a simultaneous chaos of noise, as shattered windows spewed broken glass and bricks and rubbish came thudding down on the roof of the shelter.

"They've hit the flats!" someone said.

My mother caught my arm and held me. It wasn't panic, just a protective and comforting hold – she was that kind of woman. We braced ourselves for the impending avalanche, sure that the flats would descend on us and that we would be buried under their crumbling, crushing mass. Would the shelter hold the weight? Would we be able to breathe? Perhaps we would be choked with dust and unable to call out to the rescue men to tell them where we were. These were some of the terrified thoughts that invaded my mind. I had the instinctive urge to grab my mother's hand and get out of the shelter before it all happened. But perhaps her comforting and restraining hold was her way of informing me that the entrance was already blocked. Even without the restraining hold on my arm, it was doubtful whether my legs would have the strength to carry me to the entrance, because the fear and terror within me had turned my legs to jelly. Time seemed to be suspended and motionless, almost as if it had a reluctance to proceed and to continue to bring with its passing any further extension of the present nightmare. The other people in the shelter were huddled together, grasping each other with the involuntary gesture that is inspired by unified fear. The only part of my body that was active was my churning, fear-stricken mind; the darting thoughts were a jumble of incoherent chaos.

Then suddenly the brittle limbo of time was shattered; the trance of fear was breached. I heard footsteps coming down the stairs to the shelter and bricks being kicked aside. "Is everyone all right down 'ere?" said the voice outside. The heavy curtains at the entrance were brushed aside and there stood Mr Stevens, one of our neighbours. "There's a right mess outside", he said, "but the old flats are still standing".

The surge of relief as my mind was rescued from its bonds of fear and terror is an everlasting memory of this episode. And that's all it was, just an episode in a catalogue of events that contributed to the many nights in this frightening period of the Blitz on London. This particular bomb tore a gaping hole in the middle of the road. The edge of the crater was only some twelve feet from our shelter.

We had no gas or water for a couple of weeks in our homes. My mother cooked our food on the fire and water was collected in buckets and saucepans from emergency water pipes set up in the street. During this period of the Blitz, schools in London had not yet recovered from the effects of the evacuation. Much of the schooling for the young people that remained in London was voluntary and confined to the few schools that were open. I was therefore able to remain at home and help my mother to replenish our water supply from the pipe in the street. During the next few months, there were many more long nights spent in the shelter. The coming of the dawn, which heralded the comparative safety of daylight, seemed to approach with increasing slowness. As we emerged from our concrete refuge there was always the feeling that you had survived – at least for another night. One just simply lived night by night.

## A Night in a Bermondsey Shelter
## Harry Hawes (b. 1922)

All the family documents,
an orange and some sweets,
are packed in Ma's old handbag,
with other little treats.

Carrier bags with sandwiches,
a flask of George Payne's tea,
a copy of the Standard,
and a Telfer's pie for me.

A packet of Wild Woodbines,
a bottle of Courage beer,
together with a pack of cards
and lots of other gear.

A card school in one corner,
a sing-song in another
A pretty girl with starry eyes,
is dreaming of her lover.

Women do their knitting
and menfolk study form,
others lie in makeshift beds,
trying to keep warm.

A bomber's moon shines up above
the Germans give us hell.
Wardens in their tin hats
check that all is well.

Emerging from the shelter,
feeling the worse for wear,
heading home for breakfast
*That's if it's still there.*

# We Deserved a Medal
## Lilian Blore (b. 1905)

I had two daughters who had just started school when the Second World War started in 1939. When the air raids started, one day a German plane came right down on Lewisham School and machine gunned the children sitting in their classes. To avoid that kind of thing one million three hundred thousand children had to be moved out of the Metropolitan area. Some of the children went to kent and quite a lot to the North of England. My two daughters were not evacuated, nor were all my relations' children. My two girls cried so much to stay with my husband and me that I would not let them go.

There were no schools open after a while as the war went on. The air raids began to get very severe. An air raid shelter was built next door to where I lived and all the neighbours began using it. The raids began to come every night and daytime until it became every night about 6 o'clock in the evening. They went on all through the night for ninety nights right off. The men would hardly get home from work when the siren would go. The wives would have some meals made up and something to drink. We would take some water in the shelter. We would get so dry with all the shelter closed up. No light was allowed to show out. A partition was made, with an extra large pail for the toilet. We would take our bedding. We were given two bed bunks and if there were more than four in the family you would have to manage the best way you could to sleep. It sheltered about fifty people. Some of the neighbours in the street had their own air raid shelters built in their houses.

We had some very close misses when we were in the shelter. I lost my friend and family. They had a direct hit on their shelter. The husband was found cuddling his two daughters, aged fourteen and twelve, and my friend was blown on to a roof. They were all dead. Towards the end of the war we began having Doodle-bugs, jet propelled one ton bombs. One fell quite close to me. It made my daughter Jean, a diabetic, very ill.

All railings had been removed from the streets and parks. Our railings outside our houses in Sears Street were saved, being an area to the houses. The railings went for war material. Everywhere you went you always carried your gas masks. The rations were not much. For each person you were allowed 2oz tea, 2oz margarine, 2oz butter, ½lb sugar and 1 egg with egg powder. Bread was off rations but became scarce. All offal was off rationing. Only half a rabbit was allowed in a family. The rations were for one week. My daughter Jean was allowed extra meat on her ration back as she was a diabetic. Our neighbours would pass the word around that the butcher where so-and-so was rationed had offal. You had to be quick to the shop for he would sell out. All clothes were rationed, but you could go to any shop for clothes, though you could not buy much. You would have to go very careful with your clothes. I was told after the war by a friend of mine that was on the Merchant ships that a lot had been blown up bringing food for us. He was blown up and got saved, but was terribly injured.

After the war was over all the streets had parties. We were so pleased the war was over and thanked God that peace had come. But the rationing never ended until 1952 or 1953.

I was always upset the Land Army women never got a gratuity. They worked as hard as any women in the forces and left home like other women. All the women in the forces were given a gratuity. My sister Alice's friend was in the Land Army. All privates in the forces got 2/- a day and when they were demobbed they were given £46 and a suit. The Government passed a law that all forces personnel were to be given their jobs back as soon as the war was over and they were demobilized. Nearly all the women took men's jobs over while they were in the forces. My own husband was in the Home Guard in the Second World War and my brother in law was an Air Raid Warden.

One thing I was upset over – we were never given a medal for bravery in the 1939 to 1945 War. I think myself we all went through as much as Malta.

## Home Guard
## Leslie Piper (b. 1908)

My trade of farrier kept me from the army, as we were wanted at home, horses being in demand owing to the need to conserve petrol for the war effort. Farriers over thirty years of age were, luckily for me, not called up for service.

I was a member of a small concert party and had hoped to take up singing professionally, possibly in musical shows; to this end I was taking three classes at Morley College – English, speech training and sight singing; but when the war came along my dreams were shattered. I got very little sleep once the fighting started; our concert party practices ran late and I often had to be up at three o'clock in the morning to walk over Peckham Rye, fetch a horse to the forge, shoe it, get it back again and then return to the forge to start work again at seven.

We had moved from Scylla Road to 226a Commercial Way, Peckham. It was while we were there that the Second World War was declared. Our daughter Elaine had been born a month previously in Dulwich Hospital.

I took a course in first aid and after passing my test I was posted to a heavy rescue depot for evening duty. My presence there was resented by the full time men and when the Local Defence Volunteers were formed, I left the rescue depot to join the new force.

The war made a great difference to our lives. When the air raids began, it was for me a case of work and then Home Guard duty for several evenings a week – the new force was renamed the Home Guard. Our duties at first consisted of helping the police during air raids, guarding unexploded bombs, patrolling, other guard duties and drill, lectures etc. We had to do our turn of all night duty, with two hours sentry go, and then stand by till 6 o'clock before starting another day's work. We had to snatch a few hours sleep on the floor with just a couple of blankets. Our company headquarters were usually in schools.

After one of my all night spells of duty I came home to find our house had been blasted – the front door was up the road and the windows blown out. Luckily the family were in the Anderson shelter in the garden, safe.

We found a flat in Solway Road, East Dulwich, and had just moved in by dark, when the warning went and we spent the night in the deep shelter on Peckham Rye. We had a terrible night and resolved we would never go there again, but would take our chance at home. The Anderson shelter in Solway Road was full of water; it took a lot of work to empty it and keep it reasonably dry for us to use at night.

We lived in Solway Road for a number of years and had quite a bit of minor internal damage during the remainder of the war. On one occasion the ceiling fell on me one night while in bed; I was too tired to move until the morning. Large pieces of plaster were all over the bed, which, needless to say, was in a filthy condition.

My wife Molly and Elaine had gone to live at Durrington in Wiltshire with a friend to be out of the raids. I was able to visit them once a week with a cheap pass issued by the authorities. My mother called to see me one evening as I had not been well. She left in time to get home before the air raid warning sounded, as at that period they were sounding regularly at 6 p.m. Some time later an air raid warden called to say that my mother had been knocked down at Nunhead Green and taken to hospital. He could give me no details, so I had to find out which hopsital she had been taken to. Luckily I tried Dulwich Hospital first and that was the one I wanted. These were difficult times and it was some time before they could find out if she had been admitted. When they did, I was told she was sleeping and to call again next day.

It was a wet night and the guns were firing, so it was not a very pleasant journey. My mother was moved to Caterham and then to Sutton. She had a broken leg, but the worst damage was that her mind was never quite the same again. My sister and I were sent for one night. We were told that she would never walk again and that she would be happier if she were allowed to die in her own home. They were wrong in this as she afterwards walked many miles and lived for quite a number of years.

I transferred from the Peckham to the Dulwich Company of the Home Guard, as my brother-in-law Fred and his tow sons were there. His younger son Laurie went into the army and was killed in Holland when his tank was hit and all the crew died. Ron, the older son, served in the Navy, while Fred continued as a sergeant in the Home Guard, specialising in unarmed combat. We had many terrifying experiences during the war with, after the bombers, the flying bombs and then the V2 rockets, but to recount them all would be boring to the reader as most incidents followed the same grim pattern.

The war of course brought rationing of the principal foods and of clothing. This continued with some commodities, such as meat, until well after the war. On the whole though, I think we civilians fared better with regard to food than in the First War, when I can remember lining up for hours to get a few potatoes and then often being unlucky. It was my job, too, in the first war time to line up for a bucketful of coal when the local merchant had a delivery.

The end of the war was celebrated in almost every street with a party. We had tables erected in the middle of Solway Road. With the money previously collected, plenty of food and drink was provided and all the residents sat down to enjoy themselves. Everyone was happy that the killing had stopped and that the families could be reunited.


## My Future in a Cardboard Box
## Jim Allen (b. 1915)

"I remember, I remember the house where I was born". How well I remember those lines, but I do not remember who wrote them. It is remarkable how much information is stored in that most complex of filing systems that we call the human brain. Trivial things, childhood scenes, a chance remark from a stranger, an advert on the side of a bus, are all stored in that mental larder like tins in a grocer's shop. Yet I have only a vague memory of a very monotonous part of my life: the time that I ceased to be a soldier and became a civilian, at the end of World War II. We had often wondered what the last day would be like. Old friends (age then was irrelevant) saying goodbye? But it wasn't like that. One was released according to age and service group numbers. Mine was 27 and by the time my group came up I had been shifted from pillar to post and lost and made new friends.

And so it was, on the day, a time of "organised chaos" of which I was only partly conscious, finding myself on an army truck leaving Cairo bound for England – what was left of it. Apart from a lot of movement, falling in, falling out, answering names etc, I have no idea of how I eventually found myself on board ship heading for France. I cannot remember even the name of the ship, but I know the name of the one that took us over four years earlier. Also very hazy is the time spent crossing France, except that we were on a train that had no windows or doors and so the cold and the snow swept through with savage intensity. We huddled close to each other and removed our boots so we could rub some warmth into each other's feet. It was March 1946 and cold, very cold.

We came at last to our destination, wherever it was, and after more confusion were on a small ship bound for Newhaven. It had taken ten days to reach there. it had taken nine weeks, four years previously, to get out. From Newhaven on to

Aldershot, a lot of picking up and putting down of equipment, standing still, turning left, turning right and finally being fed and watered and bedded down for the night like the good animals we were. Come the morning, March 6th, we were taken to Woking and placed in front of a counter where people with tired looking faces moved with an automatic action and asked what one's name was – again.

Now I know I should remember it all, but it's no good – I can't. It went something like this – "Name? Suit? Size? Colour?" "Suit – one; colour – blue; shirt – one; colour – white; hat – one; shoes – pairs, one; colour – brown; raincoat – one. Go to the man on the left".

I went to the man on my left. He gave me a cardboard box. "That's for your clothing. Sign here. Right, Cheerio!"

"Is that it then?"

"That's it; it's all over. Cheerio!" And, glancing at my signature, "Cheerio, Mr Allen".

Now I didn't remember ever being called Mr Allen before. I had no job to return to; I had just my army uniform, my kit bag and my new identity: my new world – in a cardboard box. I made for home – not home, but the house where my parents had been moved into after being bombed out of the home I knew. I had never been inside it. I was in a daze, but I had still the man's voice in my ears calling me "Mr Allen". That was nice. It would have been nicer if someone had said "Thank you", but they never did – I can't remember that.

# Give Us Our Day: the 1945 Election
## Alf Slater (b. 1927)

My childhood feelings about the years before the outbreak of the Second World War in 1939 were reasonably happy ones – after all, we were only kids and easily adaptable. But however young, you couldn't possibly ignore the fact that your parents, your mates' parents and most grown-ups in general were suffering great hardship. It wasn't just the poor housing or the three or four to the bed, or even the continual running battle with the hordes of invading 'livestock'. No. The despair was far more deeply rooted in a condition that is the nightmare of working people; they were unemployed. For many of them it was more than a nightmare; it was a terrible fact that, however hard they tried, there was no work for them. Many people were resigned to a hopeless future that contained no tomorrows; the results of unemployment in those days were hunger and extreme poverty. But us 'kids' weren't really aware of all this at the time, so you shared a crust and had fun.

My elder brother was a great deal older than myself. He talked to me a lot. I valued his thoughts and opinions very highly. He said to me one day, "We live in a political condition – and when people learn the difference between 'Piecrust and Promises', we'll have a better future". Those words stuck in my mind and helped to influence my thinking some years later, as I faced a working future after the War.

I was almost eighteen when the war ended in 1945. My initial feeling of relief was equally matched with one of some concern: would I be a victim of "Piecrust and Promises" and facing a future in a 'Political Condition' that put me on the corner passing a dog-end around? I soon found though, that despite the rigours and pressures of the war, the majority of people I knew were also becoming increasingly concerned about what was going to happen in their future in the Britain of tomorrow. "It's going to be different this time", were the words that were constantly expressed, particularly by older people. This was a constant reminder of the "pie-crust" promises made to them at the end of the First World War.

There was a great deal of talk about the Beveridge Plan and the Welfare State. It seemed that in 1943 a committee headed by an economist called Sir William Beveridge had produced a document for the building of the post-war Britain. It had set out in detail plans for education, a health service and pensions. This really caught the imagination of people everywhere. All that was required were the people to put this vision into practice – the political condition of the future.

It was common knowledge that a General Election was to be held in the next couple of months. There had not been an election for ten years and I was now at an age when the prospect of a change in our political condition gradually claimed my attention. With my brother's help and other forms of enlightened informa- tion, I began to form my own view as to which type of government would carry through the social reforms of the Beveridge Plan. I was too young to vote, but the desire to participate and to help in some way was compelling. There was no doubt at all in my mind that the only party capable of implementing these social reforms was the Labour Party. The leaders of the Labour Party at the time were Attlee, Bevin and Morrison. They were members of the wartime Coalition Government; they had become experienced Cabinet Ministers and had achieved a high degree of public recognition. Their support of the Beveridge Plan had not gone unnoticed among the people. Although we were sure that they were more than ready for the political battle to come, it is doubtful if they were aware of the great feeling and determination of the people for a change in the coming days of peace.

I found myself delivering leaflets and asking about voting intentions "on the knocker", as it is called. The Labour candidate for Camberwell was Freda Corbett, a lady who was eventually elected and served the people of Camberwell with great distinction for many years to come. My many enquiries left me in no doubt: the concerted mood and optimism was high.

The election of 1945 was comparatively quiet by latter day standards. The Tory Party was confident that the popularity of Winston Churchill would give them victory. Winston Churchill made an election tour of South London; he came down Walworth Road, complete with cigar and a two fingered salute. People cheered – I was among them – but he did not know then that the acclaim was for a leader of war, not the prime minister of peace.

On July the 5th, 1945, the people voted. "Vote, Vote, Vote for Freda Corbett", chanted a group of kids outside one of the polling stations in New Church Road. Feeling ran so high that my mother, an invalid, for the first time in her life was determined to vote. The result was a resounding victory for the Labour Party: an overall majority of 146 seats.

During the next few years the Labour Party of 1945 implemented the largest social reform in the history of this country. No other government this century will change the quality of life for the ordinary man or woman so much again.

I will always look upon that time as one of the most important of my young life. I had witnessed – and helped – in the birth of an era. But sadly I have also witnessed its decline and the erosion of its achievements. What went wrong? Well, that's another story.